Francois Rene Blot

The Agonising Heart

Salvation of the dying, consolation of the afflicted. Part 1

Francois Rene Blot

The Agonising Heart
Salvation of the dying, consolation of the afflicted. Part 1

ISBN/EAN: 9783337300388

Printed in Europe, USA, Canada, Australia, Japan

Cover: Foto ©Lupo / pixelio.de

More available books at **www.hansebooks.com**

THE AGONISING HEART.

ROEHAMPTON :
PRINTED BY JAMES STANLEY.

THE AGONISING HEART.

SALVATION OF THE DYING,

CONSOLATION OF THE AFFLICTED.

BY

THE REV. FATHER BLOT.

AUTHOR OF THE "AGONY OF JESUS."

With approbation of the Bishop of Mans.

PART I.

LONDON:
BURNS, OATES, & CO., PORTMAN STREET.
1869.

Approbation.

HAVING caused the work entitled the *Agonising Heart, Salvation of the Dying*, to be examined, we approve it for our diocese, and particularly recommend it to devout persons.

At Mans, October 14, 1866.

+ CHARLES, BISHOP OF MANS.

PREFACE.

On a cold snowy day in the beginning of February, 1864, the writer of these pages took a journey from Paris to Mende. This little town, the capital of the department of Lozère, is situated in a deep valley on the left bank of the Lot. Two holy men are connected with its history—St. Privat, a Bishop and Martyr of the third century, and Pope Urban V., who lived in the fourteenth century. The town takes its name from Mont Mimat, which rises near it to the height of more than 3,000 feet above the level of the sea. On the steep and barren slope of this mountain, about six hundred feet above the town, is the hermitage of St. Privat, partly cut out of the rock. The statue of the holy Pope Urban V., Bishop at once of Rome and of Mende, is soon to be erected on the "Place" in front of the ancient cathedral, whose beautiful tower is the admiration of visitors to Mende.

In this obscure valley the Divine Husbandman was pleased to sow the seed of a new Society, destined by its sweet fragrance to counteract the contagion of the sect of "Solidaires," and to bring forth most precious fruits of salvation for the dying. Godless society seeks fame and notoriety, religious society loves silence and obscurity. The aim of the one is to make men lose their souls, while the other by the most generous efforts and sacrifices seeks their salvation.

On Friday, the 5th of February, we joined the pious souls who gathered morning and evening in a poor little chapel to kindle their zeal at the Heart of Jesus, to learn something of the Agonies of the God-Man, to encourage each other in the work of helping the dying by means of prayers and charitable visits. The longing of these pure souls is to come near to the Divine Heart in the Sacrament of Its Love, and then to carry Its graces to their dying brethren. At our left hand, within a grating, was a band of virgins and widows clothed in the Religious habit; they had offered themselves to die for expiring sinners, they had given up the good things of this life, their families, their health, their very lives, in order to reconcile to God those who die each day.

In the morning we went forth, in spite of the icy wind and falling snow, to visit the dead and to kneel at the tomb of a Priest of the Society of Jesus, who had died some months before, Superior of the College at Mende. The Rev. Father Brumauld had spent twenty years in Africa, where he had been the friend of our soldiers and officers, and many of them had joined in erecting an humble but durable monument to his memory. As we rose up we saw near us a white cross, with the Heart pierced by the lance and surrounded by the crown of thorns painted on it. We learned from an inscription that beneath this wooden cross lay the mortal remains of the first Nun of the Agonising Heart of Jesus, whose vow of self-sacrifice God had heard and accepted on behalf of the dying. We were eager and happy to pray for the repose of one who had so generously prayed for the conversion of others.

In the evening, by the permission of Mgr. Foulquier, the holy and benevolent Bishop of Mans, we were admitted within the enclosure of the monastery. An account of the Community will be given in the course of this little work, which we write on behalf of the dying, having already written one on behalf of the dead, and another on the Blessed in Heaven. Perhaps, when our last hour comes, God will remember our humble efforts, and, in consideration of what we have endeavoured to do for the agonising, for the departed, and for the sorrowing survivors, will soften for us the agony which precedes death, or the expiation which follows it. Or rather— O God grant to others any consolation that might be ours, let Thy mercy comfort the afflicted, refresh the souls in Purgatory, and convert the dying, even at the cost of any sufferings or trials we may have to undergo!

The present book is divided into two parts: the first treats of Works, the second contains Prayers; the one considers the Agonising Heart more particularly as the Salvation of the Dying, the other as the Consolation of the Afflicted. These two parts might have formed a single volume, but it has been thought better to publish them separately, in order that the first may be the more easily lent and the more widely read; the second can be conveniently used by the Faithful in their private prayers, in hearing Mass in union with the Agony of our Divine Lord, in practising the Devotion of the Holy Hour for His members in their agony. This book is neither a repetition nor an abridgment of the *Agony of Jesus:* it is a supplement to it; it relates to a special work, and gives practical details necessarily omitted when the subject was treated in a more general way. We commend it to those who are seeking a remedy for their sorrows, to those who would win for their relations and friends the great grace of a holy death. It will put before you a work of the greatest importance, and specially favoured by Providence, a work of prayer and suffering for the benefit of the dying, in which you may cooperate, and while promoting their salvation, find comfort and light for your own souls.

The greatest things often spring from small beginnings. What was but a speck on the horizon becomes a cloud, bearing refreshment or devastation to the whole country. When Israel had sinned and forsaken the true God, for three years there was neither dew nor rain, and then a cloud not bigger than a man's footprint rose out of the sea. The Prophet Elias foretold a great rain, and soon the heavens grew dark and it fell in torrents. Alas! the withering effects of impiety and forgetfulness of God are to be seen around us on every side! How many souls are scorched by evil passions and profanity! Who will give them back some of their former freshness? Who will pour down on them a shower of grace from the treasures amassed by the Blood and Tears and Sufferings of the Son of God? This is the office of the Devotion to the Agonising Heart of our Saviour. Its beginning was small and almost imperceptible, in the middle of this century, hidden in the breast of a humble recluse; and even when it appeared above the horizon, it seemed at first but a speck. Now, however, the entire Church is overspread with it; blessings and graces are pouring down on the whole world, the afflicted are being consoled, the dying are being saved; each day fresh fruits are brought forth, and we see Christians from all ranks of society, laymen as well as Religious of contemplative and active Orders, children of St. Vincent of Paul and disciples of St. Ignatius, joining in a common and generous Devotion to the interests of the dying.

Saint-Germain-en-Laye, December 27, 1865,
Feast of St. John the Evangelist.

TABLE OF CONTENTS.

PREFACE . . . . pp. vii—xiii.

I.—THE DEVOTION.

CHAPTER I.
REMOTE ORIGIN OF THE DEVOTION TO THE AGONISING HEART OF JESUS.

Explanation. Remote origin of this Devotion found in the Incarnation, and especially in the Agony in the Garden. Mary the first to practise it. All pure souls have with St. John imitated her compassionate Heart. Meaning of the practices. Devotion to the Sacred Heart its source. Its name is not new, nor is it new in its highest expression, *i.e.*, the renunciation of the world . . . . pp. 1—9.

CHAPTER II.
PROXIMATE ORIGIN.

Devotion to the Mystery of the Garden of Olives developed in our days. Its preparation in Paris at the Rue des Postes. Its formation at Vals près le Puys. Approbation given by Pius IX. at Naples. First pamphlet published at Avignon . . pp. 9—16.

CHAPTER III.
NATURE OF THIS DEVOTION.

Object of veneration, object of supplication. First aim of Devotion to the Sacred Heart *to honour;* second aim *to repair.* Both attained by Devotion to the Agonising Heart. Usefulness of the Devotion, a usefulness distinct from that of the Bona Mors. The four fruits of a good work . . . . . . pp. 17—23.

CHAPTER IV.
THE OBJECT OF OUR VENERATION.

Devotion to the Agonising Heart forms a link between Devotion to the Sacred Heart and Devotion to the Holy Agony. The Agony of the Heart of Jesus explained by French authors. This Agony caused by the sight of our sins, by compassion for our miseries, and by the foreknowledge of Its own sufferings. Our preachers often represent sin as inflicting Agony on the Heart of Jesus. Greatness of this Agony . pp. 24—32.

CHAPTER V.
ADVANTAGES OF THIS DEVOTION.

Social utility of every Catholic Devotion. Fruitfulness of Devotion to the Heart of Jesus. It is reasonable to honour the Agonising Heart. It is just to give It thanks. It is useful to pray to It. Charity in the Garden of the Church . . . . pp. 32—40.

CHAPTER VI.
LET US CONSOLE THE AGONISING HEART OF JESUS.

We console It by imitation. By converting the dying. How much the sight of the lost afflicted It. How much the sight of our efforts consoles It . pp. 40—46

CHAPTER VII.

THE OBJECT OF OUR SUPPLICATIONS.

Devotion to the Heart of Jesus an excellent preparation for a holy death. The Agonising Heart invoked for the salvation of the dying. The last agony. Terrors of the dying sinner. We cannot perfectly describe the last agony, but we can sanctify it by prayers . pp. 47—55.

CHAPTER VIII.

LET US NOT FORSAKE THE DYING.

In former times every Christian prepared for death. Works on this subject. But now the dying often will not even see a Priest. Touching prayer of a dying Religious that the dying may not be forsaken. Let us be their visible angels . . . . pp. 55—60.

CHAPTER IX.

REASONS FOR HASTE.

Reasons of our prayers for the dying. Jesus asks it of us. We pay homage to His Agony when we trust them to His Agonising Heart. Time presses. Let our assistance be in proportion to the necessity for it. Let us be apostles. Let us pray by working and by suffering. We shall be prayed for in our turn . . pp. 60—65.

II.—THE CONFRATERNITY.

CHAPTER I.

OLD ASSOCIATIONS FOR THE RELIEF OF THE DYING.

Influence of the Association. The holy women on Calvary. The service of the hospitals, and of the ministers of the sick. Confraternity of the Holy Agony of our Lord. Bona Mors under the protection of the holy Angels. Confraternity of St. Francis of Sales for the agonising . . . . pp 66—73.

CHAPTER II.

THE NEW ASSOCIATION SUITED TO THE PRESENT TIME.

Fitness of devotion to the Agonising Heart, as regards its object of veneration and its object of supplication. Prayer is often our only way of promoting the salvation of the dying. The association of the "Solidaires" and its motto. Episcopal condemnation. Support from Freemasonry. Opposition to this satanic society becomes a necessity. Mission of the Associates of the Agonising Heart. An ingenious method adopted . . . . pp. 74—82.

CHAPTER III.

PROGRESS OF THE WORK.

Short prayer to the Agonising Heart distributed everywhere, like a blessed seed. Benevolent assistance of pious persons. Association established at Bourges, at Mans, at Niort, and Limoges. Interior progress of the work, or greater perfection of means. How the Association may be established . . pp. 83—88.

CHAPTER IV.

VISITING THE SICK.

Recommended by the Founder. The first Confraternity of Charity and the society of ladies established by St. Vincent of Paul for the purpose of visiting the sick. Much good is still done in Paris by this society. The Association of the Agonising Heart promotes the same work. Statutes relative to visiting the sick. How God leads founders and developes their undertakings . . . . pp. 88—94.

TABLE OF CONTENTS. xix

CHAPTER V.
PRAYER AND ACTION.
Variety in unity. Contemplative and active Nuns. Apostolic Society of the Sacred Heart. Prayer is the soul of the Society. And action combined with prayer and suffering is its ordinary means . . pp. 95—102.

CHAPTER VI.
THE WORK IN COMMUNITIES.
This work flourishes best in Communities, because their members are most like Jesus in His Agony. The resemblance strengthened by devotion to His Agonising Heart. Zeal of active Communities for our object; and of contemplative Communities , pp. 102—107.

CHAPTER VII.
GRACES OBTAINED THROUGH IT.
Blessings connected with the worship of the Sacred Heart. Blessings received by the Associates of the Agonising Heart. Their special happiness in Heaven. Graces which they gain for others. Examples . pp. 107—112.

CHAPTER VIII.
THE DYING CONVERTED.
Conversion of two old men, one rich and the other poor, one at home and the other in a hospital . pp. 112—128.

CHAPTER IX.
OTHER EXAMPLES.
Conversion of a young man who had resisted grace. Conversion of an impious blasphemer. Reflections of a Religious . , . . . pp. 118—124.

CHAPTER X.

ARCHCONFRATERNITY AT JERUSALEM.

All hearts are turned towards Jerusalem. A young person invokes the Agonising Heart for her dying father; causes a medal to be struck; wishes for the establishment of an Archconfraternity at Jerusalem; corresponds with Father Lyonnard. The Patriarch, Mgr. Valerga, views the project with favour. Its execution delayed by difficulties . . . . . pp. 124—129.

CHAPTER XI.

ARCHCONFRATERNITY AT JERUSALEM.

Decree of the Patriarch establishing the Confraternity. Indulgences granted by the Pope. How to become a member. First consequence, propagation of Devotion to the Agonising Heart. Second consequence, the diffusion of the general Devotion to the Sacred Heart. Egotism and self-indulgence will be thus diminished by this Devotion . . . . . pp. 130—139.

III.—THE COMMUNITY.

CHAPTER L

CONTEMPLATIVE CONGREGATION OF THE AGONISING HEART.

The work of the Agonising Heart is glorious. Usefulness of the contemplative life. Its principle and its object—love of man and love of God. The more contemplative Orders love God, the more they love their neighbours. Contemplative Communities increase devotion and love. This will be specially true of the Community of the Agonising Heart . pp. 140—146.

CHAPTER II.
IDEA OF THE FOUNDATION.

The Foundress' attraction for Religious life. She is left a widow with ten children; devotes herself to the care of the sick; builds a chapel in honour of the Agonising Heart; wishes to establish a Community; speaks of her desire to Father Lyonnard; and resolves to undertake it . . . . . . pp. 146—152.

CHAPTER III.
EXECUTION OF THE PROJECT.

The first vocation. Departure for Mende. Token of the divine pleasure by a miraculous cure. Opening of the Novitiate. Death of the first Choir Sister. The Foundress and two Sisters take their vows. Paternal care of Providence. The House at Lyons . pp. 152—160.

CHAPTER IV.
ABRIDGED FORMULARY OF THE INSTITUTE.

Object, vows, cloister, prayer, mortification, work, dowry, auxiliaries, spirit, devotion. Apostolic object often set before the Religious. Prayers for the direction of the intention. The Community meet present needs. It will maintain the Devotion and the Confraternity . . . . . . pp. 161—166.

CHAPTER V.
THE VOW OF IMMOLATION.

Its obligations. Offering of life. God has often accepted this kind of offering. Value of this vow. Resemblance which it produces between Jesus Christ and the Religious. Its power for good . . pp. 166—172.

CHAPTER VI.
THE CONSTITUTIONS.

Object of the vocation. Spirit of the Institute. Cloister. Postulate. First Novitiate. Second Novitiate. Form of Profession. Question of Conscience . pp. 173—178.

CHAPTER VII.
A DAY.

The cell. The Religious dress. Act of offering. Psalmody. Mass. Manual labour. Meals. Recreation. Rosary. Intercession. Homage to the Dying Saviour's Agony . . . . pp. 179—186.

CHAPTER VIII.
A PROFESSION.

St. Agnes, model of all virgins who consecrate themselves to the Lord. Preface sung by the Celebrant. Words sung by the virgins. Special observance at the Profession in honour of the Agony of our Lord. Peculiarities in the ceremony of giving the Religious dress . . . . . . pp. 186—193.

CHAPTER IX.
DIFFERENT REPRESENTATIONS OF THE AGONY OF JESUS.

The new Institute represents the Saviour's Agony. Material representation. Historical representation. Moral representation . . . . pp. 193—198.

CHAPTER X.
MYSTICAL REPRESENTATION.

Exercise of the Five Wounds. Exercises of reparation. The Holy Hour. Oblation — Intercession — Fast. Humiliation in the refectory. Prayer to the Angel of Consolation . . . . . pp. 198—204.

CHAPTER XI.

DEVOTION TO THE COMPASSIONATE HEART OF MARY.

Honours paid to the Blessed Virgin. Daily prayer. Consecration made on Saturday. Exercises of humiliation on her seven principal Feasts. Zeal of Mary for the salvation of the agonising. Let us imitate this zeal . . . . pp. 204—210.

CHAPTER XII.

THE SALVATION OF THE AGONISING.

The good that women can do by a hidden life. A cloistered Nun has sometimes been chosen by God to cooperate with an Apostolic man. Usefulness of the Nuns of the Agonising Heart, especially to the dying . . . . . . pp. 210—216.

CHAPTER XIII.

PRAYERS OF CONTEMPLATIVE ORDERS.

Detractors of contemplative life inconsistent and unjust. Good done by contemplative Orders. Examples of sinners converted by them. Value of the prayers of a whole Community . . . . pp. 216—221.

CHAPTER XIV.

CONVERSIONS OBTAINED.

Conversion of a merchant at Mende. Conversion of an old man in the diocese of Bordeaux. Holy deaths of the relations of Nuns. To multiply conversions let us promote the extension of the Society . pp. 222—227.

CHAPTER XV.

THE FUTURE.

Providential designs. The spirit of prayer and contemplation is kept alive amongst us by the contemplative Orders. The Agonising Heart of Jesus will revive it among the active Orders. Perhaps it may become a common centre of prayer for all. The active spiritual life, or mixed life, will be developed; this is the most perfect of all. The work will become a great and fruitful tree . . . . . pp. 228—234.

PRAYERS FOR THE DYING.

I. Daily Prayer (Latin and English) . . 235
II. Litany of Jesus in the Garden of Olives . 236
III. Litany of St. Joseph 238
IV. Prayer of a Nun of the Visitation . . 240
V. Prayer of Father Franco 243
VI. Prayers of Morvelli 243
VII. Prayers of Lattaignant 245
VIII. Litany of the Dying 246
IX. Recommendation of a Departing soul . . 248

THE AGONISING HEART.

I.—THE DEVOTION.

CHAPTER I.

REMOTE ORIGIN OF THE DEVOTION TO THE AGONISING HEART OF JESUS.

Explanation. Remote origin of this Devotion found in the Incarnation, and especially in the Agony in the Garden. Mary the first to practise it. All pure souls have with St. John imitated her compassionate Heart. Meaning of the practices. Devotion to the Sacred Heart its source. Its name is not new, nor is it new in its highest expression, *i.e.*, the renunciation of the world.

THE Incarnation itself is the remote origin of the Devotion to the Agonising Heart. The moment that the Eternal Word took Flesh in the womb of the Blessed Virgin Mary, that Mother learned the mystery of His future sorrows, and sympathised with the anguish caused by our sins to the Heart of the Divine Child. The Heart of Jesus was in Agony from the very hour of His Conception, and from that hour Mary shared the Agony of her Son, and thus won her beautiful name—"Our Lady of the Sacred Heart." In the first work ever written on these two Sacred Hearts, we read, "As soon as the Blessed Virgin became the Mother of our Redeemer, an undying struggle of love began in her Heart; on the one hand she knew that it was the will of God that her beloved Son should suffer and die for our salvation, and her ardent love for the Divine Will and for the salvation of souls wrought in her a perfect submission to this decree; but, on the other hand, her surpassing maternal love caused her unspeakable anguish at the sight of the torments which her most dear Son was to undergo for the redemption of the world."*

Holy Scripture, however, only uses the word "agony" to express the mental sufferings of the Man-God on the Mount of Olives. Mary underwent an agony like that of Jesus, because of her love and her compassion, or rather, her devotion for Him. Our author adds, "The Saviour having bid farewell to His most holy Mother, plunged into an immense ocean of sorrow; and His desolate Mother, wrapt in contemplation, shared them in her Heart. Thus that sad day was for her a day of prayer, of tears, of interior agony, of perfect submission to the divine will; and from her inmost soul

* Eudes, *Le Cœur Admirable*, t. ii., l. vi., cap. v.

also arose those words which He spoke in the Garden of Olives, "Father, not My will but Thine be done."*

Mary's devotion to Jesus in His Agony never failed. St. John the Beloved, who has been called the first Disciple of the Sacred Heart, rested on his Master's Bosom amid the joys of the Eucharistic Banquet, but during His fearful Agony on the Mount of Olives, like James his brother, like Peter his chief, he yielded to sleep, and thus incurred that Master's reproaches; while Mary had the glory of being for the time the only Disciple, the most constant companion, the best consoler of the Agonising Heart of Jesus. It was that most faithful Virgin who, by her example more than by her words, led the virgin Disciple to Calvary's height, where he stood with her at the foot of the Cross, with her compassioned the dying Saviour's Agony, and with her entered by force of love into the Sacred Heart, there opened by the soldier's lance. From the time of the faithful Disciple all pure souls have longed to be with Mary in her desolation, all Saints have shared with her the sufferings of her Divine Son. They have placed their hearts beneath His Heart, to be purified by the Water and vivified by the Blood; they have taken up their abode in that open Heart as in a sure place of refuge. With the Mother of Dolours they

* Eudes, *Le Cœur Admirable*, t. ii., l. vi., cap. v.

have watched the Agony of her Son in the Garden of Olives; they have joined in her devotion to His Agonising Heart. What Saint is there who has not found a subject of deep and constant meditation and compassion in the interior anguish, the mental sorrows, the hidden Passion endured by Him from His Incarnation to His Death? The depth of affliction into which our sins plunged His Divine Heart, His sympathy for our miseries, His perfect knowledge of the outrages committed against His Father, of the torments He was to undergo, have ever been matter of adoring study and contemplation to pious and faithful Christians. They have turned to Gethsemani when oppressed with fears and cares and sadness, and the Agonised Heart of their Good Master has been their refuge and their hope. In proof of this we need only refer to the quotations we have made in the *Agony of Jesus.*

Looking on this Devotion as consisting in special practices, we find the germ first springing up, the beautiful rose-bud beginning to open, at the very time when, under the pious care of Father Eudes and from revelations made to Blessed Margaret Mary, the Devotion to the Sacred Heart filled the world with its fragrance. One Devotion contains the other, just as the "genus" contains the "species;" one produces the other, as the same branch often produces several flowers. Are not Devotion to the

Agonising Heart and Devotion to the Eucharistic Heart the fairest flowers that spring from the general Devotion to the Divine Heart of Jesus, which the one honours in Its present state, and the other in Its past? The special Devotion to our Saviour's Agony may then be traced at least to those two chosen souls, whose whole life on earth seems to have been but one long agony.

About the year 1660 Father Eudes composed a Mass and Office for the Feast of the Sacred Heart, which were approved by several Bishops. In 1672 he ordered that the Feast should be celebrated on the 20th of October by all the Religious of his Congregation. In his circular letter he forestalls an objection which might be raised to this Devotion of the Agonising Heart. "If," says he, "the novelty of this Devotion is objected to, I answer that novelty, though most dangerous in matters of faith, is very good in matters of devotion. Otherwise we must rescind all the Feasts of the Church which were once new, and especially the later ones, such as the Feast of the Blessed Sacrament, of the Holy Name of Jesus, of the Immaculate Conception of the Blessed Virgin, of her Name, and many others which have been added to the Roman Breviary.*

In the following year, 1673, one Friday, after Holy Communion, Margaret Mary received the

* De Montigny, *Vie du P. Eudes*, l. x., p. 368.

first revelation regarding the "Holy Hour." She was directed always to rise in the night between Thursday and Friday, and to honour the Agony suffered by our Lord in the night of His Passion, by saying certain prayers which He Himself indicated. This pious practice made its way, though it was long opposed by Margaret's Superiors. "Certainly," says her historian, "that blessed one is well recompensed for all she went through when, looking down from Heaven, she sees every week, at the same hour that the Saviour, prostrate before His Father, watered the earth with His Blood, so many pious souls deny themselves the repose of sleep, and conquer the weakness of the flesh, that they at least may escape the reproach addressed to the first witnesses of His Agony—"What! could you not watch with Me one hour?"*

Devotion to the Agonising Heart of Jesus is not then new in this, one of its principal practices, any more than in its substance or in its source. The very name is not new, for it is found in a Latin work, by Ginther, approved in the year 1705, and called the *Mirror of Love and Grief in the most Sacred and Divine Heart of Jesus*, from which we proceed to quote : "So overpowering was the weight of fear and sadness which pressed on that most loving Heart in the

* Daniel, *Histoire de la B. Marguerite Marie*, cap. x., p. 112.

Garden of Olives, that the hearts of all men, if they had been joined together, could not have borne it, but must have broken at once. Was it not meet that the King of Martyrs should show us in His own Person what the Martyrs have suffered, or rather what they would have had to suffer, unless He had upheld them and consoled them by His grace? And can you yourselves consider the Heart of Jesus agonising in Gethsemani—*Cor Jesús agonisans* —without being touched to your very heart's core by compassion for Him, and contrition for your sins? How will it be with you if some day an agony like that oppresses your own heart? How much more severely will you judge your present life, your coldness, your want of devotion? How will you feel if the coming judgment and the eternal punishment you deserve appear before your agonising heart —*agonisanti cordi tuo.*"* "The Prophet Jeremias, with the Agony of the Heart of Jesus before him, wrote—'My heart is poured out upon the earth'— my heart, where life has its source, where the blood is purified, where the affections dwell. For was it not on the Mount of Olives that the Heart of Jesus poured forth Blood? And if the Eternal Father requires such an expiation from the Heart of His Son for sins not His own, what will become of you, who

* Ginther, *Speculum Amoris et Doloris*, consid. xxxi., nn. 5, 6.

have committed so many? Who will be able to bear his own sins, when our Creator and Saviour is sorrowful even unto death, and trembles and falls under the weight of the sins of others—*ad mortem usque SS. Cor Ejus agonisat ?* "*

The Devotion of which we treat is not new in its highest signification—that renunciation of the world in honour of the Agony of the Divine Heart practised at the present moment by the Sisters of the Sacred Agony and the Nuns of the Agonising Heart. Our author gives an example from the earliest ages of Christianity. Theodore, a rich and noble youth, lived in Egypt in the midst of luxury. One day his eye was caught by a representation of Jesus in the Garden of Olives, and at the same moment grace touched his heart. He fell on his knees, and with many tears besought our Lord to bring him into the way of salvation and of perfection. His mother did her best to detain him, but the Saviour's sweat of blood gave him courage and strength. He bade farewell to the world, to his relations, his wealth and pleasures, and withdrew to a vast desert, to imitate his Agonising Lord by a life of continual prayer and voluntary mortification.†

We read of this same St. Theodore in the

* Ginther, *Speculum Amoris et Doloris*, consid. xxxiii., nn. 2, 3.
† *Ibid.*, consid. xxxi., n. 6.

life of St. Pacomius,* whom he succeeded as spiritual guide of his Monks. St. Nilus, Gennadius, and Cassian, also speak in his praise.† One single sight of the Agonising Heart of Jesus was his first step towards that eminent holiness which he afterwards attained. Can we wonder if that sight still produces the same effects? And must not the sight of the living images of His Agony, of those generous beings who honour and revive its remembrance in these mournful mysteries, inspire others with the same desire, the same abnegation, and the same devotedness?

CHAPTER II.

PROXIMATE ORIGIN.

Devotion to the Mystery of the Garden of Olives developed in our days. Its preparation in Paris at the Rue des Postes. Its formation at Vals près le Puys. Approbation given by Pius IX. at Naples. First pamphlet published at Avignon.

DEVOTION to the Agonising Heart of Jesus is new only in certain practices, and in the favours granted by the Sovereign Pontiff to those who adopt it. That Providence which has reserved

---

* *De Vitis Patrum.*, l. i.; *Vita Sancti Pachomii*, capp. xxix., xxx., xxxi.; Migne, *Patrologie Latine*, t. lxxiii.
† St. Nilus, *De Oratione*, cap. cviii.; Gennadius, *Liber de Scriptoribus Ecclesiasticis*, cap. viii.; Cassian, *De Cœnobiorum institut*, l. v., cap. xxxiii.; *Collatio* vi.

for these later times the manifestation of all the treasures of grace contained in the Sacred Heart, has willed also that in our age of agony, at the very epoch of our greatest calamities, Devotion to the Agonising Heart should be fully developed. It appears as a token of hope, a rainbow in the midst of the storm, inviting sorrowful souls to put their confidence in God, to turn for consolation to the Heart of their Good Master, and to draw from the never-failing fountain of His Agonies salvation for all who are in their last agony.

On the 29th of August, 1828, Leo XII. gave permission for a special Feast, and approved of a service and Mass in honour of our Lord's Prayer on the Mount of Olives; and on the 27th of July, 1831, Gregory XVI. granted indulgences to the members of the Confraternity of the "Holy Hour."

During the scholastic year of 1843—4, a young Religious of the Society of Jesus, destined by Providence to be instrumental in the establishment of this Devotion, was studying literature in a house in Paris (18, Rue des Postes), where love of the Sacred Heart is an undying tradition. During the last century it was inhabited by the disciples of Father Eudes, and after the Great Revolution by the Nuns of the Visitation, Sisters of the Blessed Margaret Mary.* In 1830 one part of the house (No. 24

* *Vie de P. Eudes*, l. ix. fin, p. 361.

in the same street) was the Office of the Catholic Association of the Sacred Heart, which published the *Life of the Blessed Margaret Mary Alacoque,* and *Devotion to the Sacred Hearts of Jesus and Mary; or, the Salvation of France,* with many other works of piety. At the time of which we speak, this house had been for some few years the residence of the Fathers of the Society of Jesus. Fathers Barat and Varin, founders of the congregation of instruction so well known by the name of the Sacred Heart, spent their last days there. There also Father Daniel wrote his *History of the Blessed Margaret Mary,* and there we ourselves made the first outline of these volumes on the Agonising Heart. May not this uninterrupted tradition be a reason for blessings granted, for successes gained by the many young men of good family who are now prepared in this house for the Government schools? At any rate, there is no spot in the capital where a magnificent sanctuary of the Sacred Heart might more fitly be erected in commemoration of many benefits.

A little chapel near the street was often visited by him whom God was preparing to lead men to know and invoke the compassionate Heart of Mary and the Agonising Heart of Jesus. The grace that prepared him was a grace of interior suffering, of mental pain, which became very intense during the following year. After these sharp trials, the thought of the Agonising Heart of Jesus and the compassionate Heart of Mary came clearly before his mind. While Devotion to the compassionate Heart of the Mother was to bring down from Heaven to earth the graces needed by the living for their comfort, and for the sanctification of their own sorrows, Devotion to the Agonising Heart of the Son was to be a noble vessel, rescuing the shipwrecked, and bearing those who die each day from the shores of time to the haven of a happy eternity.

In the order of grace, as well as in that of nature, there is a wonderful system of connection; the most beautiful creations of Christian genius are not isolated, others have prepared the way for them, or accompany them, and they all render assistance to each other. Again, it may be remarked that as nature prepares for certain plants a favoured soil, specially fitted to bring them to the greatest perfection, so grace chooses for the birthplaces of its noblest works spots which have already been sanctified by peculiar devotion and great virtues. At the very time of which we speak, the same house sheltered another Religious, who was hereafter to propagate Devotion to the Sacred Heart, and the Apostolate of Prayer. The two met again at Vals près le Puys, where Devotion to the Agonising Heart took a definite form.

This important seminary has constantly sent forth intrepid Apostles to the conquest of souls in all parts of the world, and Providence was now bringing together and preparing materials for fresh works which were to radiate from the same centre. It was here that the Rev. Father Gautrelet composed a book on that Apostolate of Prayer, which has been so happily developed by the talent and zeal of Father Ramière. Its monthly publication, the *Messenger of the Sacred Heart*, spreads a practical love of the Heart of Jesus, together with much information regarding its interests, throughout all ranks of society. Once every year is read in the Refectory at Vals a short notice of Charles Bertrand, who died there about this time in the odour of sanctity, after having shared in the blessings showered down upon that holy house. His vocation was that of a victim for the good of others, and he was the first who was buried in that cemetery where other Brothers of St. Francis Xavier have since wished to have a resting-place. Is there not a fruitful Apostleship in suffering, longed for with a holy longing, and in the lot of a victim patiently borne? Do not many sinners owe their conversion to conflicts, anguish, and agonies silently endured by generous hearts? The Devotion to the Agonising Heart of Jesus for the salvation of those who die each day, unites in itself these two Apostolates of Prayer and of Suffering, as is shown by its Founder in his excellent book, the *Apostolate of Suffering*. The idea took its final form in his mind while he was still a Deacon, studying theology at Vals. It was not, he says, due to his own industry or his own reflections. God made use of him for the growth of this Devotion in the field of the Church, just as He makes use of the ground where the grain of wheat falls from the hand of the sower. Time passes, and on the day and at the hour appointed by God, the blade silently springs up.

Before the Very Rev. Father Roothaan, General of the Society of Jesus, was obliged by the Revolution of 1848 to leave Rome, he received the confidence of our humble Religious, who wrote to him, enclosing a letter which he begged him to present in person to His Holiness. The most Rev. Father, so well known for his learning and wisdom, approved of the Devotion, became its promoter with the Head of the Church, and adopted the custom of saying three times a day this prayer, which expresses its object and its aim: "O most merciful Jesus, lover of souls, I pray Thee by the Agony of Thy most Sacred Heart, and by the sorrows of thine Immaculate Mother, cleanse in Thine own Blood the sinners who are now in their last agony, and are to die this day. Amen."

"O Heart of Jesus, once in Agony, pity the dying!"

By the Decree, which we cite, given at Naples, in the suburb of Portici, on the 2nd of

February, 1850, Pius IX. attached indulgences to this short prayer. "As it is appointed to every man once to die, and as an eternity of glory in Heaven, or an eternity of torment in hell, depends on the moment of death, it is well that all the Faithful of Jesus Christ should often offer up pious supplications to God, the Father of Mercies, imploring for those who have come to their last moment, and are about to expire, the aid of His divine grace, without which it is impossible to enter into eternal life. And it will come to pass that in His infinite goodness the Lord will grant the same mercy to those who during their life have performed this office of charity for the dying. Wherefore our Holy Father, Pius IX., in order to incite faithful Christians more and more to practise this pious exercise of prayer for the dying, and in consideration of the supplications which have been made, that he would open the sacred treasury of indulgences for this purpose, has been pleased to grant to all the Faithful of both sexes, an indulgence of a hundred days every time they recite with contrition and devotion the prayer beginning 'O most merciful Jesus,' and the versicle 'Heart of Jesus,' in any language, provided the translation be correct. But to those who with the same dispositions, say this prayer and versicle at three different times in the day during a full month, our Holy Father the Pope, with the same goodness, grants a plenary indulgence on any day that may be chosen, on condition of previous contrition, confession, Communion, and prayer of some minutes for his intentions, in a church or public oratory. These indulgences are granted for ever, and are applicable to the Faithful departed."

On the 22nd of July in the same year, two treatises published at Avignon by the Rev. Father Lyonnard, who then lived there, were approved by Mgr. Debelay, Archbishop of Avignon, and pronounced well fitted to revive faith and piety among Christians. They are entitled *Devotion to the Agonising Heart of Jesus*, and *Devotion to the Compassionate Heart of Mary*. These works were offered to Pius IX., who was pleased to acknowledge them by Mgr. Fioravanti from Rome, on the 3rd of April, 1852, in these words: "The Sovereign Pontiff Pius IX. has received your letter, and the copy of the book which you have written in order to promote among the Faithful devotion to the Sacred Hearts of Jesus and Mary. He desires me to thank you for this present, and he duly commends the religious zeal with which you recal to the veneration of Christians the Sorrow and the Passion of Christ our Redeemer, and of the most holy Virgin His Mother. To this mark of his favour His Holiness is pleased to add his Apostolic benediction, which he bestows affectionately on you for the welfare of your body and your soul."

CHAPTER III.

NATURE OF THIS DEVOTION.

Object of veneration, object of supplication. First aim of Devotion to the Sacred Heart *to honour;* second aim *to repair.* Both attained by Devotion to the Agonising Heart. Usefulness of the Devotion, a usefulness distinct from that of the Bona Mors. The four fruits of a good work.

AT the beginning of the first chapter of his book on this Devotion, the author thus explains its nature : " The practice which we suggest to the piety of the Faithful consists in daily offering a short prayer to the Agonising Heart of Jesus, in order to obtain the grace of a good death for those of every age and sex, of every country and religion, who daily pass from this world into eternity, to the number of about 80,000. This practice has a double object, an object of *veneration* and an object of *supplication.* The object of veneration is the interior suffering of the Heart of Jesus, the kind of Agony which it underwent during His whole mortal life, and especially in the Garden of Olives. The object of supplication is to gain from that same Heart the grace of a holy death for those throughout the whole world who are in their last agony, those who must die each day. This short summary is sufficient to explain the nature of the practice, and no words of ours are needed to show its excellence."

Father de Galliffet defined Devotion to the Sacred Heart as "an exercise of religion whose object is the adorable Heart of Jesus Christ burning with love for men, whose aim is to honour that Divine Heart by every homage that love and gratitude can suggest, and more particularly to make reparation for the injuries which He receives in the Sacrament of His love."* Father Eudes appears only to have had the first aim, *honour*, directly in view. "What solemnity," he exclaims, "can be more holy than this, which is the very principle of all that is great, holy, and venerable in all other solemnities? What heart can be more worthy of adoration, of love, and of admiration, than the Heart of the God-Man? What honour is due to that Heart, which has ever rendered, and will throughout all eternity continue to render, more glory and love to God at every moment than all the hearts of Angels and of men could render during all eternity; that Heart which is occupied day and night with doing us infinite good, and which was broken on the Cross by Its excess of love for us!"† The Blessed Margaret Mary had the second aim, of *reparation*, specially in view, and our Lord wished her above all to repair the outrages which are offered to Him in the Eucharist. He said to

---

* De Galliffet, *De l'Excellence de la Dévotion au Cœur Adorable de Jésus Christ*, l. i., cap. iv., 3.
† *Vie du P. Eudes*, l. x., p. 368.

her: "I would have the first Friday after the Octave of the Blessed Sacrament sanctified as a particular Feast, that My Heart may be honoured by Communions, and by an honourable reparation of the indignities which It has suffered since It has dwelt on the altar."*

The preceding passages clearly show how far the Devotion to the Agonising Heart resembles the Devotion to the Sacred Heart, and where they differ. They have two objects in common, the honour of the Heart of Jesus, and the reparation of the outrages which It has suffered from men.

The Devotion to the Agonising Heart grows from the general Devotion to the Sacred Heart, as the branch from the tree, joined to it and yet distinct from it. The Heart of Jesus is ever one and the same, but this Devotion has one especial aspect—Its past, not Its present state; Its mortal, not Its sacramental or glorious life. It honours those continual inward griefs by which It was formerly oppressed, and above all Its Agony in the Garden of Olives. The reparation is also special in its character. It is not a direct reparation of the outrages endured by the Sacred Heart in the Eucharist, though indeed some part of the long Agony of the Heart of Jesus was caused by the dying who refuse the Holy Viaticum. It is simply a reparation of *the* great outrage, the most cruel of all

* *Memoires de la Vie de la B. Marguerite Marie*, n. 54.

that can be offered to that loving Heart, the outrage of those who despise Its love, Its graces, and benefits, who *will* die in impenitence and lose their souls, to redeem which every drop of Its Blood was shed.

But the reparation thus offered to the Agonising Heart of the Saviour is most pleasing to Him, and invaluable to us. It forestalls the evil in order to prevent it, instead of following it slowly in order to efface its stains. And as the most perfect manner of redemption is that which the Son of God employed in regard of the creature who was to be His Mother, by preserving her from even the original taint of sin, so the most perfect reparation for the thousands of sinners who die each day is one which rescues them from final impenitence, instead of merely seeking to console the Heart of Jesus for their eternal damnation.

It cannot then be said that this Devotion is a needless addition to the many works of our day which prove so short-lived, either because they are not needed, or either because their origin cannot be sufficiently traced to past ages. In its purpose it is as old as the world, as wide as human nature, as durable as the Church militant, for death belongs to all times and all places, and many men, alas! are in danger of dying as they have lived, far from God, and from the way of salvation. As to its means, it seconds the constant solicitude and the principal effort of the Church, whose object is to obtain, by prayer and suffering, as well as by energetic action, that the just may end a good life by a still better death, and for sinners, that they may meet death in such a way that it may atone in some degree for the sinfulness of their lives. "Perhaps," adds the author of this Devotion, "it may be said that our practice is useless, because its purpose is already realised by the Confraternity of the Bona Mors. But a moment's reflection suffices to do away with this objection. For, not to dwell on the different nature of the homage which each of these Associations renders to our Lord (the Confraternity of the Bona Mors not taking the Sacred Heart as its special object of veneration), is there not a most manifest difference between the practical aims of each? The most worthy and excellent Confraternity of the Bona Mors has for its end the good death of its own members. It is circumscribed by local limits. The Association of the Agonising Heart, on the contrary, aims at obtaining a good death for all who are in their last agony throughout the whole world. It is Catholic in the literal sense of the word, for by prayers it embraces not only the dying of one country, one Association, or one family, but the dying of the universe, rich and poor, great and small, the believer and the unbeliever. Moreover, it is for those who are actually dying this very day, hence the daily prayer which is prescribed as its fundamental practice. There is, therefore, a real distinction between the Confraternity of the Bona Mors and the Association in honour of the Agonising Heart of Jesus; the one is a means by which the Faithful may prepare themselves for that last passage, the other is a means by which they may prepare others. It is ruled by a spirit of zeal. It desires, by the help of God, to do for the dying a work similar to that which the Propagation of the Faith does for the heathen, that is, to gain the grace of salvation for them by daily supplication, as that other admirable Association, by means of its weekly alms, added to the prayers of its members, endeavours to gain for unbelievers the divine gift of faith.*

Not only by prayer, but also by every action of our lives, we may honour the Agonising Heart of Jesus, and contribute to the salvation of those who die each day. Every good work performed in a state of grace produces four kinds of fruit. The first is merit, and this merit belongs to the Christian who performs it. Then there is satisfaction, and this satisfaction may be applied by way of assistance to our departed friends. In the third place there is glory to our Lord and the Saints, and this glory may be directed by our intention to the Agonising Heart of the Son of God. The last fruit is

* Lyonnard, *La Devotion au Cœur Agonisant de Jésus*, cap. vii.

one of impetration; it obtains grace for the living, whether they be righteous or sinners, and this fruit may be applied to the poor souls who die every day, to win for them the graces of conversion, salvation, and final perseverance.

Such is the vast field which lies before the pious members of our Association. Each step they take in the right way, each act of virtue they perform, however small it may be, adds something to their own personal merits for all eternity, and also consoles the Heart of Jesus in Its Agony, and helps to complete the harvest of the Elect, on which He has spent His labours, His griefs, and His bloody sweat. May we not truly say, "The harvest indeed is great, but the labourers are few. Pray ye therefore the Lord of the harvest, that He may send forth labourers into His harvest." Pray to Jesus in His Agony, pray to His Divine Heart, and bestir yourselves with zeal and perseverance, in order to recruit labourers, members of this Association, from all ranks and from all ages.

CHAPTER IV.

THE OBJECT OF OUR VENERATION.

Devotion to the Agonising Heart forms a link between Devotion to the Sacred Heart and Devotion to the Holy Agony. The Agony of the Heart of Jesus explained by French authors. This Agony caused by the sight of our sins, by compassion for our miseries, and by the foreknowledge of Its own sufferings. Our preachers often represent sin as inflicting Agony on the Heart of Jesus. Greatness of this Agony.

As we have already seen, this Devotion presents the Agonising Heart of the Divine Master to our veneration. By this very act it united itself to the Devotion to the Sacred Heart and the Devotion to the Holy Agony. This connection has often been pointed out by pious authors who have dwelt on all the afflictions of the God-Man, especially His Agony on the Mount of Olives, as centred in His Heart. How often when they speak of His interior sufferings is His Heart mentioned! This may be observed in almost every page of the *Agony of Jesus*, where we have purposely placed a capital at the beginning of the word, as often as it refers to our Divine Lord. It may be observed that these three kindred Devotions sprung up in France, by a merciful design of Providence in favour of a nation which is full of heart and generosity, yet hurried on to many miseries by carelessness and religious indifference. French authors are those who have most constantly referred all the Agonies of Jesus to His Sacred Heart. We cite some passages, not so much in proof of this, as for the sake of making the object of our veneration better known. Father Guilloré, of the Society of Jesus, writes thus: "His Heart was constantly wounded afresh, and His Soul was always oppressed with the deepest sadness. O poor, forsaken, agonising soul!"* Another Religious of the same Order says: "He was first wounded in His Heart; O God, what agony to suffer thirty years in His Heart what He was at last to suffer in every member of His Body!"† The Founder of the Oratory, Cardinal de Bérulle, had already said: "His Heart was pierced by grief before It was pierced by the lance. That grief overwhelmed It in life, and the lance pierced It in death."‡ Father Eudes, the Founder of the Congregation of Jesus and Mary, goes into further details :—

"Our sins are the first cause of the most grievous wounds of the Divine Heart of our Redeemer. I have read in the life of St. Catharine of Genoa, that one day God showed to her the horrible nature of the smallest venial sin,

* Guilloré, *Conférences Spirituelles*, l. i., conf. iii., sec. 3; *Des Maximes Spirituelles*, t. i., l. iii., maxime xviii., cap. ii.
† Ragon, *Le Calvaire*, entretien iv., p. 2, n. vii.
‡ De Bérulle, *Œuvres*, Paris, 1665; *Œuvres de Piété*, n. lxvii.

D

and she assures us that though the sight lasted only one moment, it was so fearful, that the blood froze in her veins, she felt as if she were in her last agony, and must have died, but that God miraculously preserved her to tell others what she had seen. She further said, that were she plunged in an abyss of fire and flames, and were escape offered to her on condition of beholding that sight again, she would remain where she was rather than again encounter it. Now, if the sight of the smallest venial sin was so terrible to the Saint, what must we think of the state to which our Saviour was reduced by the sight of all the sins of the universe? For they were all continually before His eyes, and inasmuch as His insight was infinitely clearer than St. Catharine's, they appeared infinitely more horrible to Him. The sight of these sins pierced His Heart with innumerable wounds. Count, if you can, all the sins of men, which are greater in number than the drops of water in the sea, and then you may count the wounds of the loving Heart of Jesus."*

"The second cause of these wounds is the infinite love of that Heart for all Its children, and the sight of all their troubles and afflictions, especially the torments of the holy Martyrs. When a tender mother sees a child suffer, she feels the pain even more acutely than he does. Our Lord loves us so much, that if the love of

* Eudes, *Le Cœur Admirable*, t. i., l. vi., cap. i.

all fathers and mothers were gathered into one heart, it would not equal one spark of that love which burns for us in His Heart. Therefore, all our sorrows and griefs being ever clearly and distinctly present before His eyes, were so many bleeding wounds in His paternal Heart, wounds so deep and so painful that they would have caused His death thousands and thousands of times during His life, and even at the very moment of His birth, unless that life had been miraculously preserved, for during its whole course His Heart was pierced by all these mortal wounds. All the crosses and afflictions of His children converged towards His tender Heart, as towards their centre, and no mind can understand the martyrdom It has suffered. Oh, how truly may It be called the King of Martyrs, the Centre of the Cross! Oh, what consolation for the afflicted in the knowledge that all their afflictions have passed through the most benign Heart of Jesus, and that He has first borne them for their sakes!"*

On the Feast of St. John the Evangelist, 1674, Blessed Margaret Mary had a vision which bears on the same subject. "The Heart of Jesus," she says, "appeared to me upon a fiery throne, It radiated light on every side, It was more brilliant than the sun, and clear as crystal. The Wound which It received on the Cross was visible; a crown of thorns surrounded

* Eudes, 8me *Meditation.*

It, and a cross seemed to stand on It. My Divine Master let me know that these instruments of His Passion meant that the immense love of His Heart for men had been the source of all His sufferings; that from the first instant of His Incarnation all these torments had been present to Him, that from the first moment the Cross was, so to speak, planted in His Heart; that He then accepted all the griefs and humiliations to be suffered by His Holy Humanity during His mortal life, as well as all the outrages to which His love for men would expose Him, by remaining with them for ever in the Blessed Sacrament."*

Thus the object of our veneration, the adorable Heart of Jesus, was always agonised on three accounts—(1.) horror of sin, which is an outrage to God; (2.) compassion for the ills which afflict men; and (3.) foresight of Its own sufferings. Our preachers have not spoken of the second; of the third they only say, "Jesus sees all the torments He is to suffer, He has in His Heart the Cross and Mount Calvary, the synagogue and the conduct of the Romans;"† but the first has been developed at length. "Man sinned first by his heart, and so Jesus is first punished in His Heart—where sin began in the one, the penalty begins in the other. The Heart of Jesus was crucified in the Garden,

---

* Languet, *La Vie de la B. Marguerite Marie*, l. vii.
† Bouzeis, *Sermon* x. *sur la Passion*.

before His Body was crucified on Mount Calvary, by a crucifixion even more severe, because sin employed more hands to perform it."* "His Heart writhes, and is transformed and melted at the sight before him."†

"Without this interior Agony, the satisfaction of Jesus Christ would not have been complete. The sufferings of His Body were destined to expiate the transgressions of our bodies, the licence of our looks was to be effaced by His Tears, the sensuality of our repasts by the bitter gall that was offered to Him, the vanity of our attire by the thorns on His Head, the idleness of our conversations by His rigorous silence in the midst of torments; but, after all, these things are but the outward part, the body of sin; reparation must be made for the inner man by the interior sufferings of Jesus Christ, the secret transgressions of our heart and mind must be expiated by the Agony of His. It is on account of the criminal joys on which your heart loves to dwell, its continual dissipation among the pleasures of the world, the satisfaction you sometimes find in your very faults, that the Heart of Jesus is overwhelmed with sorrow. It is because of the deadly security in which you live, steeped as you are in sinfulness, that the Soul of Jesus is oppressed. It is for

---

* Hubert, *Sermon pour le Vendredi Saint*, 2e point.
† G. Terrasson, *Sermon pour le Vendredi Saint*, 1er point.

the subtle pride of seemingly pious people, for the secret enmities fostered by the vindictive, for the impure thoughts of the voluptuous, for the evil motives of hypocrites—in a word, for all spiritual sins, that the Heart of Jesus Christ is sorrowful unto death."* "As the sin of Adam had its beginning in the depths of his heart, before it was actually committed, so the greatest sufferings of the Son of God were graven in His Heart; and in the Garden of Olives he endured a Passion of the Soul scarcely shared by the Passion of the Body, but which will increase in process of time and in the same proportion as sin, for which it is the remedy, grows, extends, and is multiplied after it has once arisen in the human heart. The sorrow of Jesus Christ begins in His Heart; it will continue till it comes to perfection, and that perfection will be the Death of the Victim. His Soul is bowed down with sorrow, for as Adam's sin began by secret pride His Passion begins by a sadness which weighs down His Soul. It is to be observed that He declares His sadness, not to His Father, but to His Disciples, to show us that it is at once a sacrifice and a lesson. He teaches us where our penitence must begin if it is to be true—even in the depths of our hearts. For, the will being the principle and source of our actions, we are

* De la Roche, *Sermon pour le Vendredi de la Semaine Sainte*, 3e point.

sinners in so far as our will is opposed to God and rises against Him; we are real penitents only when it submits and when the heart is changed."*

How great was the Agony of the Heart of Jesus from these manifold causes! No one can imagine it, and Christian orators of former ages have vainly tried to give an idea of it.

He who was associated in the work of Blessed Margaret Mary, exclaims, "O incomprehensible grief, incredible bitterness of the Heart of Jesus, rendering Him insensible to sufferings so violent, making them even seem to Him a kind of solace. Yes, in each torture inflicted on the Son of God, the Soul has had a thousand times greater share than the Body."† Another preacher of the same period says, "Tormentors, you cannot touch the living Heart of Jesus Christ. His Head indeed is given up to your thorns, His Shoulders to your scourges, His Feet and Hands to your nails, but as for the living Heart of a God, it is God alone Who can pierce It with grief."‡ A little later we find these words from Father la Pesse, "We may adore His Agonising Heart, and call Him, in

---

* Dom Jerome, *Sermon pour le Vendredi Saint*, 1er partie.
† De la Colombière, *Sermon pour le jour de la Passion*, 1er partie.
‡ De Fromentières, *Sermon* ii. *pour le Vendredi Saint*, 1er partie.

the words of the Prophet (Isaias liii. 3), *Virum dolorum, scientem infirmitatem* — "A Man of sorrows, Who is full of the sufferings He is enduring."* And Perusseau adds, "The Heart of Jesus was crucified in the Garden of Olives before His Body was crucified on the Mountain of Calvary, and the Cross in the Garden was bitterer than the Cross on the Mountain."† Lastly, another preacher of the Society of Jesus, Perrin, speaks of the Anguish and the Bloody Sweat of Gethsemane as a cruel and a sanguinary sacrifice, in which the Heart of Jesus is at once Priest, Altar, and Victim.‡

CHAPTER V.

ADVANTAGES OF THIS DEVOTION.

Social utility of every Catholic devotion. Fruitfulness of Devotion to the Heart of Jesus. It is reasonable to honour the Agonising Heart. It is just to give It thanks. It is useful to pray to It. Charity in the Garden of the Church.

ALL the quotations which we have made in the preceding chapter are from authors of the last two centuries. It is, then, no new custom to bring the Agonising Heart of the God-Man before the Faithful as an object of their love

* La Pesse, *Sermon* lxvii. *sur la Passion*, 1er partie.
† Perusseau, *Sermon* xv. *de la Passion*, 1er point.
‡ Perrin, *Sermon* xxxii. *sur la Passion*, 1er partie.

and worship. Such veneration could not long remain barren, for everything in the Church, whether it be of the nature of pious custom or of holy doctrine, has its social utility. The age in which we live required a proof of this, and we ought to endeavour to increase such veneration.

The Beloved Disciple of the Heart of Jesus, the Apostle St. John, saw a clear river proceeding from the Throne of the Lamb of God, and on both sides of the river the tree of life, yielding its fruits every month, for the healing of the nations (Apoc. xxii. 1, 2). What is the Throne of the Lamb of God amongst us? The altar, the tabernacle, where He really abides, where He receives our homage. What is the clear river proceeding from it? The river of all the graces contained in the Eucharist, the river of all the sacraments. And what are the two trees of life growing one on each side of this torrent of graces? The Sacred Heart of Mary and the Sacred Heart of Jesus, which have ever made the earth produce fruits of salvation, and which even at the moment when the condition of nations seemed most hopeless have blossomed afresh to restore them to health and to hope. How many useful works have arisen and have prospered under the protection of the adorable Hearts of Jesus and Mary! What may we not expect, in these days of affliction, from the Agonising Heart of the Son and the compassionate Heart of the Mother? That tree of life planted by the torrent of all graces, the Divine Heart of the Son of Mary, says to us, "I am the Vine, you are the branches; he that abideth in Me and I in him, the same beareth much fruit" (John xv. 5). What is it that sends through the branches the vital sap, without which they would be barren? Each pulsation of the Heart of Jesus. What is it which suits their fruitfulness to the needs of the time, producing a beneficent variety? The Heart of Jesus, ever more lavish of its treasure as the world becomes more selfish, more inflamed with love as charity grows colder. Under Its strong and sweet influence numbers of men and women have been found ready to practise self-abnegation and devotion to their neighbours. They have given up the joys of an earthly family to form spiritual families, where, by their instruction and training, they have led little ones to share in the blessings of the Sacred Heart; by the work of the Apostolic Ministry they have brought sinners back to Its love, and by contemplation they have joined in the homage which it constantly renders to God. Though still in the world, the Faithful of all classes gather constantly round the altar, to adore, to love, and to imitate the gentle and humble Heart of Jesus, as truly present in the consecrated Host as in the Bosom of His glorified Human Form in Heaven. Therefore there is a rich and touching variety in the works and devotions which love for the Heart of Jesus constantly originates. How eagerly, for example, is the Communion of Reparation everywhere adopted, because it consoles at once the Heart of the Son and the Heart of the Mother!

But after having considered the Heart of Jesus as a whole, zeal for Its glory necessarily proceeds to contemplate the divine masterpiece in Its different aspects, with a view of offering to each a special honour. The subject is inexhaustible, and its infinite variety in unity will be the eternal admiration of the Blessed in Heaven, as it is already our happiness on earth. The Faithful have been invited, in the *Annals of the Blessed Sacrament* (1860),* to offer to the Eucharistic Heart of Jesus a perpetual adoration of thanksgivings and reparations. A sanctuary has been raised in Its honour, and prayers have been approved and circulated. In accordance with the pious wishes of the generous person who wrote that invitation, built the chapel, and distributed the prayers, we mean this year to publish a treatise called *The Eucharistic Heart*. It is indeed the same Sacred Heart that has already been honoured, for the Divine Master has made known His desire that a special reparation should be offered for the

* *Annales du S. Sacrement*, t. ii., p. 325—352, Avril, 1860.

outrages that He receives in the Sacrament of the Altar,* but the form of that honour was not hitherto so definite or the homage so complete. So again, although the Agonies of the God-Man and the martyrdom of His Heart have always been an object of worship, the moment was to come when that worship was to be more peculiar and distinct, and to have a special aim of its own.

Is it not reasonable to honour the Agonising Heart of Jesus? We are not content with honouring His Humanity in general, but we pay particular honour to each member of His Sacred Body, which has been tortured for our sakes. The Five Wounds of our Lord, the Crown of Thorns, the Lance, the Nails, the Precious Blood, the Cross, the Holy Winding Sheet, each painful instrument of our redemption has become the object of a special Feast. Does it not follow as a legitimate consequence that we ought to venerate that which suffered the most, which contributed most largely to our salvation, and is in Itself the most worthy of our adoration, I mean the very Heart of the Redeemer—that Heart which has suffered so much only because It has loved us so much? The physical sufferings of our Saviour were surpassed in intensity and in duration by His mental sufferings.

Is it not just to give thanks to the Agonising

* Daniel, *Histoire de la B. Marguerite Marie*, cap. xii.

Heart of Jesus, seeing that by the merit of Its past sufferings we enjoy infinite benefits, and by the never-failing virtue of its surpassing Agonies we are encouraged, consoled, and fortified? When trouble overtakes us, when inward sorrows oppress us, when our heart is ready to break under the weight of Its burden, where shall we seek for refuge, save in the Arms of Jesus hanging in agony on the Cross? Where shall we look for help and support but in the Heart of Jesus suffering Agonies in the Garden of Olives? Where shall we turn for light and consolation but to the example of Jesus in Agony throughout His whole life? Everything is out of sorts in our present state of society; the earth brings forth thorns, the vineyard bears no fruit for Heaven, virtues are tainted by a corrupt atmosphere, but is not Jesus with His suffering Heart bending over us like the good Samaritan, and pouring oil and vinegar into our wounds? Is He not here to water the earth again, to make the vineyard fruitful, and to give forth a sweet perfume like the rose of Jericho? Let us show Him our gratitude, and respond to the following invitation addressed to the Faithful early in the last century: "Christian soul, behold and consider how much the Heart of Jesus has suffered for you. Come to the Mount of Olives, and behold the new Adam, watering the earth with the sweat of His Brow, with His own Blood, that it may bring forth fruit. Look at the Beloved Son of the Eternal Father painfully cultivating this barren vineyard, and refreshing it with a dew of Blood, that at last it may rejoice the eye of its Master. Behold this Cypress Grape before He is bruised in the winepress of the Cross, yielding of its own accord the wine of virgins, and dyeing His robe, the Church, in that precious stream. Tears and fragrance are distilled from that mystical Rose of Jericho by the fire of love that burns in the Heart of Jesus, and the odour of sweetness rises to the throne of the Heavenly Father for the salvation of the world. This Good Samaritan. at the outset of His sad Passion, bows Himself to the earth, where poor human nature is helplessly lying wounded, on its way to Heaven, by infernal thieves; He pours oil and wine into our wounds, as a healing balm and a remedy against death. Most holy and loving Heart, who can help sharing Thy sadness? who can fail to be touched with compassion for Thee? O Jesus, my Love, I am guilty, and Thou dost suffer! With what depth of gratitude ought not my heart to be filled."*

Is it not useful to pray to the Agonising Heart of Jesus for the afflicted and for the dying? In so doing we console His sorrow, we draw unlimited benedictions from an ocean of graces, we practice charity towards God and

* Ginther, *Speculum Amoris et Doloris*, consid. xxxiii., n. 6.

towards our neighbour. The ardent intercessions of countless souls, the help which they gain for the wretched, show that they have their part in that spiritual Priesthood of which the Scriptures speak when they call the Faithful a "holy nation" (Exod. xix. 6), "the kingly Priesthood" (1 Peter ii. 9), "Kings and Priests" (Apoc. v. 10). Is not suffering itself a priesthood, when resignation makes our heart like the Heart of Jesus, at once altar, Priest, and victim? How can it fail to be fruitful, when it unites itself by prayer to the most loving of all hearts? If we love to place flowers around His image, or His earthly tabernacle, must we not long still more to gather souls from destruction, that they may shine around His Heavenly throne, like living and beautiful blossoms?

The Church is a mystical garden, watered by the Blood of Calvary, and the tears of Gethsemane, and death comes there daily to collect flowers for God and the Angels. Alas! how many are not worthy to be offered to our Lord, and are only fit to be cast into the fire like vile weeds! The scorching heat of passion, the worm of sin, the blast of a worldly, dissipated life, have blighted and withered them in the sight of God. What will give them back a little of their freshness and glory, that death may not cast them into the eternal fire? Praying love, active and suffering love, united in devotion to the Agonising Heart of Jesus! Prayer fills the fountains, whence patience and action draw water to refresh these fading flowers. The gardener who has a clear running stream at his command can do much to restore the beauty of his flowers by watering them every evening. And so in the evening of life our dear dying ones must be refreshed before the dark night hides them from our eyes. How happy and beautiful will they be when they meet us in the eternal light of day, if by our efforts they have succeeded in coming to Jesus Christ! Oh, Agonising Heart of our Good Master, what a triumph for Thee, what a joy for us! Oh, give us, we beseech Thee, zeal, and active compassion, and a spirit of prayer, that we may pay Thee the homage of consoling Thee by our veneration of Thy Holy Name!

CHAPTER VI.

LET US CONSOLE THE AGONISING HEART OF JESUS.

We console It by imitation. By converting the dying. How much the sight of the lost afflicted It. How much the sight of our efforts consoles It.

FROM the earliest days of the Christian Church, compassionate souls in all ranks of society have gathered round the Man of Sorrows to adore Him by becoming His angels of consolation.

And how have they consoled Him? By resemblance and by zeal; by their care to imitate Him and bear Him company in His sorrows and His desolation, and by their efforts to bring back the strayed sheep whose wanderings have been the chief cause of His Agony.

By the agony of renunciation and poverty, by the agony of desolation and loneliness, by the agony of humiliation and contempt—in short, by resemblance to our Agonising Lord, do we bear Him company in His Anguish, and enter into His very Heart. A poor and humble girl, known by the name of the good Armelle, who had for years suffered a spiritual agony, speaks on this subject in words which we will quote; and let us not blame her mode of expression, for when our Lord speaks to one of His creatures, He condescends to adapt Himself to the limits of its intelligence and the simplicity of its heart.

"I found myself," she says, "dwelling in the Sacred Heart of Jesus, with such love, and glory, and liberty, that I could not understand it. I was free and at my ease. I saw that this Divine Heart was so large, that a thousand worlds would not fill It. I saw that all those who dwell there by love enjoy true and entire liberty, and wondrous peace; but on the other hand, I saw that the door was so small, and so narrow, that very few could come in. In astonishment I said, 'Oh, my Love and my All, whence comes it that Thy Heart is so large and spacious, and yet the door of entrance so small and narrow?' Then our Lord made it known to me that it was because He would have none but the *little*, the *naked*, and the *lonely* enter there. The *little* are those who with all their heart become lowly and humble for love of Him; they can enter, but others cannot; for how can a person who is great and puffed up with self-esteem pass through so small a door? The *naked* are those who withdraw their hearts from the desire of the riches and comforts of this life; as for those who are laden with bundles of gold and silver, or other things, it is impossible for them to pass through such a narrow opening. The *lonely* are those who cut off their love from all creatures; for love binds the heart to its object, and two persons who are bound together cannot enter at once where there is barely room for one."*

And what are the three causes which most frequently plunge us into a state of extreme suffering? Humiliation, which makes us *little;* losses, which leave us *naked;* abandonment, which makes us *lonely*. To be abased, to lose one's goods, to be forsaken, these are graces which the Agonising Heart of Jesus bestows on us, to make us like Him. But they are not received with gratitude or resignation, save by

* *La Vie de la bonne Armelle*, par Jeanne de la Nativité, Ursuline, l. i., ch. xxi., n. 8.

souls devoted to His Agony, compassionate and generous enough to wish really to resemble Him and be with Him.

Zeal for the conversion of the dying consoles the Agonising Heart of Jesus; for the cause of His most cruel sufferings was the distinct sight of the lost. By His infallible foreknowledge and tender love, our Saviour had the Agony of all those sinners who die impenitent, and incur eternal punishment, present to His sight. "How could the most loving, and most pitiful of all hearts, be insensible to so overwhelming a spectacle? David, in the grief of his heart at the death of an ungrateful and rebellious son, cries out, 'My son Absalom! Absalom, my son! would that I might die for thee!' (2 Kings xviii. 33). St. Paul, changed from a persecutor to an Apostle, suffers as it were the pains of travail till Christ be formed in the souls confided to his care (Gal. iv. 19). Every day we see how mothers sacrifice themselves to mere natural affection, how they watch by the sick beds of their children, how they are worn with grief at the very thought of losing them. And can the Word of God, made Man to save us, the only Son of a Father who is Love Itself, and a Mother who is incarnate charity, can He be without pity and compassion for the miserable multitudes who are daily on the very brink of destruction? The sight saddens *us*, must it not have rent the loving Heart of our gentle

Saviour? No one doubts that the evil life of a sinner afflicts the Heart of Jesus. But if this sinner is converted at the hour of death, a reparation is made which consoles Him; at least He has not the pain of seeing that His sufferings are useless. But if a life of iniquity continues to the last moment, if the sinner dies in final impenitence, then indeed the Heart of Jesus must have been overwhelmed with grief. Oh, my Divine Master, we know too little of the deep wound made in Thy Heart by this sad thought of the future, by the sight of so many souls who are determined to despise Thy love, and to perish for ever! From Thy childhood this sword pierced Thy holy soul."*

Our Lord Himself condescended to make the following revelation to the Blessed Varani: "Oh, how cruelly My Heart was torn by the sight of so many lost souls, so many members wrenched from My Body, never to be reunited to Me their Head! *Never*, that fatal *never*, will be through all eternity the greatest of all possible torments to those wretched souls. And to Me what can be more sorrowful than that *never?* Ah! how willingly would I again have suffered all those separations, with all imaginable pains —and that not once, but an infinite number of times—for the joy of seeing, I say not all, but even a single one of those souls restored to the number of My living members, of those Elect

* *Dévotion au Cœur Agonisant de Jésus*, ch. iii.

who will live eternally by a life proceeding from Me, the very Life of all the living. Learn then how dear to Me are the souls of men, since I would have suffered so much to bring one back to Me. And know also that, by reason of My justice, this '*never*' is so terrible to the lost that there is not one amongst them who would not be ready to endure the torments of a thousand hells at once for the hope of being reunited to Me in the most distant of future ages. But it can never be, and this is the fulness of their misery, the most fearful of their sufferings. The punishments in store for human iniquities are proportioned by My strict justice to the pain which each mortal sin has inflicted on My Heart. Eternity has no torture like that pitiless '*never.*' This consideration applies to all sins without exception. Behold, then, My daughter, behold and consider how My soul was rent, even till the very moment of death, by the sight of the multitude of the lost who were all at once before My sight."*

Therefore we ought to console Jesus in His Agony, not only by following His example in our sufferings, but also by our zeal for the conversion of the dying. He saw all our sins during His Agony, but He also saw our efforts, and as He was then saddened by the faults we are now committing, so He found consolation

* B. Varani, *Traité des Douleurs intérieures de Jésus Christ*, ch. i.

in the conversions we are now obtaining. While He suffered unspeakable Agony in the Garden of Olives, His Divine Father sent an Angel from Heaven to strengthen Him (Luke xxii. 43). Was He, then, so completely abandoned on the Cross as to have none to console Him? "Not so," replies a pious author, "but He who comforted Him in the Garden by an Angel comforted Him on the Cross by the penitent thief (Luke xxiii. 42). The conversion of that malefactor, the salvation of one soul rescued by His Blood from the flames of hell, consoled our dying Saviour more than all the Angelic choirs could have done had they left Heaven and gathered round His Cross."* His Passion was not in vain; in that one converted sinner our Saviour saw all the sinners who turn to Him at their last moment, and when His Heart was opened by the lance, Paradise was opened for them by His mercy and love. The more we multiply conversions among the dying the more we multiply the consolations of our Divine Master. If you would be angels of consolation to His Agony, then, become apostles to His dying creatures.

* Ginther, *Speculum Amoris et Doloris*, consid. xix., n. 5.

CHAPTER VII.

THE OBJECT OF OUR SUPPLICATIONS.

Devotion to the Heart of Jesus an excellent preparation for a holy death. The Agonising Heart invoked for the salvation of the dying. The last agony. Terrors of the dying sinner. We cannot perfectly describe the last agony, but we can sanctify it by prayers.

DEVOTION to the Agonising Heart of Jesus has for the object of its supplication the eternal salvation of those who die each day. There is a fitness in this, for must not the dying Saviour be disposed to show special mercy and compassion to the dying? And has not devotion to His Sacred Heart ever been a token of predestination, an excellent preparation for a holy death?

Let us quote Father Eudes and the Blessed Margaret Mary, two names which we love and associate for their common glory, as well as for the honour of his disciples and of her sisters. "The Nun of the Visitation," says her biographer, "received from on high a special mission, marked with a miraculous character— it was that of confidant and authorised interpreter of the Heart of Jesus." At the same time, the Founder of the Eudistes, following the impulses of his devotion, had been preparing the hearts of the Faithful to listen to the appeals of the Divine Heart. We read in his life: "Besides the annual Retreat, which he never omitted, he generally spent ten days at another time of the year in a series of pious exercises which formed a preparation for death. In the year 1673 he wrote a memorandum, which he put in a place known to his brethren, begging them to open it in the event of his serious illness. It was an instruction as to the means he wished them to employ to prepare him for a good death. He specially urged them to have the sacraments administered while he retained the perfect use of his reason. He wished to gain all the indulgences for the hour of death attached to medals and to the recitation of certain prayers. He begged that in case he should lose consciousness before having made all the acts of his preparation for death, some one else should pronounce them for him in his presence, most particularly the acts of faith, and of that entire submission to the decisions of authority which characterises the true children of the Church. His concluding wish shows his tender piety. He desired (we give his own words) 'that the grains of dust into which his miserable body should be dissolved might become so many hearts and tongues to praise God, to love and glorify the Sacred Hearts of Jesus and Mary, and to adore and bless the Holy Trinity for the treasure bestowed on his Congregation by the gift of those adorable Hearts.' "*

* De Montigny, *Vie du P. Eudes*, l. x.

The Blessed Daughter of St. Francis of Sales writes: — "Secular persons will find in this Adorable Heart their place of refuge during life, and, above all, at the hour of death. How sweet is death to those who have had a constant devotion to the Sacred Heart of Him Who is to be our Judge!"* She herself furnishes a proof of this. She wished to prepare herself to appear before God by a Retreat of forty days, and we have the record of her sentiments of confidence and love: "I purpose to make a Retreat in the Sacred Heart of Jesus Christ. I expect and hope for all the merciful help I require. I have put my whole trust in Him, for His great goodness has never disappointed me when I have turned to him; on the contrary, it seems pleasing to Him to have to deal with a creature as wretched and miserable and needy as I am, that He may bestow His infinite riches on my poverty. Only let me love Thee eternally, O my God, and then do with me what Thou wilt. I am insolvent— Thou seest it, my Divine Master. Put me in prison, I am ready, but let it be in Thy Sacred Heart; and when I am there keep me captive, bound by the chains of Thy love, till I have paid Thee all I owe. And as I can never do this, I never wish to leave my prison." When death approached she begged those around her to say the Litanies of the Heart of Jesus, and

* Languet, *Vie de la B. Marguerite Marie*, l. vi., fin.

she exclaimed—"Yes, I hope that by the love of the Heart of Jesus we shall go to the house of the Lord, and *that* before long. I want nothing but only God, and I would lose myself eternally in the Heart of Jesus Christ."*

In the progress of the general Devotion to the Sacred Heart a moment naturally came when the Faithful began specially to invoke the Agonising Heart of their good Master, to obtain a holy last agony for themselves or for others. The great thing to be gained for multitudes of sinners daily summoned by death into the presence of their Judge is an agonising heart, agonising with penitence, agonising with a real, supernatural, great and universal sorrow, like the sorrow of the Heart of Jesus in the Garden of Olives. What an undertaking! What a work! How earnestly ought we to turn to the Saviour's Agonising Heart and pray Him, in the name of the dying—*Cor mundum crea in me, Deus* (Psalm i. 12). O God, create in me an agonising heart, for only by agony can my heart be pure! It must be bruised and broken by contrition before it can follow Thee to Heaven, where nothing enters that is not perfectly pure.

The grace of final perseverance is placed so high that it can only be won by great efforts of prayer and supplication. No one can merit it for himself, no one can secure it for another, save by a particular favour of God. And how

---

* Languet, *Vie de la B. Marguerite Marie*, l. ix.

can we obtain such a favour except by long and earnest prayers, like those of our Saviour in His Agony? Therefore the Church has constantly urged on the Faithful fervent prayer for the salvation of the dying, and for this purpose the agonies of death have been often portrayed to them. St. Ephrem, Deacon of Edessa in the fourth century, spoke thus: "Do you not see what terrible things happen to the dying? What sighs they heave? They are bathed in sweat like labourers in the harvest-field, but it is a cold and deadly sweat. How restlessly they turn their eyes! how they gnash their teeth! Some rave, some are in a state of torpor and of terror. Some tear their hair, some rush from their beds and wish to flee, but they cannot. They see things they have never seen before, they hear what they have never heard before, they suffer what they have never suffered before. They seek a deliverer and no one delivers them, they seek companions and no one accompanies them, they seek an advocate and no one dares to defend them. We weep and tremble with them, we hold their hands, we embrace them, we shed tears over them, we wipe the sweat from their brow and the tears from their eyes, we give them a little water to cool their burning tongue, we put our ear to their lips in order to catch their feeble words. Then we say to them, 'How are you now? Fear not, God is goodness itself.' This is what we say to them in a voice choked with tears, and such scenes make our hearts burn within us. We think no more of impure love, of avarice, of the pleasures of the table. But in sight of the great and fearful mystery of death we tremble, we shake our head, our countenance becomes downcast, we think ourselves truly wretched, we weep over our miserable condition, exclaiming, 'Woe! woe! woe!'"* In the seventeenth century Richard l'Avocat thus described the fears of a sinner in his last agony :—" What terrors seize on those who are dying laden with unrepented sins ! The sins of their life, the pains of death, the danger of hell, are three causes of their sad state. A time will come when the soul will reproach itself for its unfaithfulness, when sins for which it has had no real sorrow will overwhelm it. Formerly they were like foul and corrupt waters, stagnant in the heart, but a time is coming when they will rise and break their bounds and become torrents to trouble us (Psalm xvii. 5), bringing back in a fearful manner the memory of our past negligencies, throwing us into a state of consternation, perhaps even of despair. That time is the time of the last agony. Oh, the terrible affliction, the dreadful anguish of the last moments of a soul unfaithful to the graces of its vocation! It is afflicted by the remembrance of sins, and

---

* St. Ephrem, *Sermo in eos qui in Christo Obdormierunt*, tom. iii., p. 263. Edit. Assemani.

by the interior upbraidings of God. As death approaches sin changes its appearance—it gives death a sting which penetrates the inmost soul of the sinner (1 Cor. xv. 56). Without sin death would have no terrors, with sin it is full of terrors; without sin a man would die content, like just old Simeon, with sin he dies like wretched Cain, who could not escape the wrath of God; without sin death is the sleep of the predestinate, with sin it is the beginning of the torments of the damned; without sin the pains of death are easy, with sin they are fearful and desperate.

"Do not mistake apparent for true conversion. The one is merely the effect of nature, which cries, and complains, and sees the cause of its sufferings, like the unhappy Antiochus (2 Macab. ix. 13). The other is an effect of grace, a work of the Most High, implying on the sinner's part free-will and compunction of heart. But where is the free-will of a dying man? Where is his real compunction? What is to become of his poor soul? Where will it go? 'The sorrows of death compassed me, and the perils of hell have found me' (Ps. cxiv. 3). He used to see that place of torment afar off, but now he must see it near at hand. He used only to think of it from time to time, for there were many other things to distract his mind, now he cannot forget it. 'Hell hath enlarged herself, and opened her mouth without any bounds' (Isa. v. 14). All things now are changed, the axe is laid to the root of the tree; a terrible voice from Heaven cries out that it is to be cut down (Dan. iv. 11), that it has cumbered the ground too long. Death comes nearer every moment; the natural heat forsakes the body, the limbs are bathed in cold perspiration, branches are already cut off, nothing is left save a few leaves on the barren trunk. What is it fit for? 'Cast it into the fire!' is the awful sentence of our Lord (John xv. 6). I do not dwell on the violent temptations and on the awful apparitions which increase the horrors of the sinner's agony. Fearful sights surround him and drive him to despair, and his own conscience becomes at once his accuser and his tormentor; on the one hand are his past sins; on the other are the devils, who are only waiting for his last breath to seize upon him; above him is an implacable and justly indignant Judge; beneath him are the flames of hell, ready to swallow him up,. and behind him is the world, urging him on to death, that death which will separate soul from body, and give him up as a prey to his enemies throughout an eternity of woe."*

Perhaps the description is incomplete. But who can fully portray the physical and moral

---

* Richard l'Avocat, *Supplíment au Dictionnaire Moral,* dis. xx., *sur les frayeurs des pécheurs à l'agonie,* 1er point.

agony of death? We have no special revelations on this subject, as we have with regard to Purgatory. Who has returned from the gates of death with perfect memory of his sufferings there? Who has even approached them without losing consciousness and feeling? No doubt this is the reason why so much less is said of the dying than of our dear departed ones. But we have been urged to pray for the dead and for the dying; and especially to commend the dying to that Divine Saviour, Who knows by His own experience what the death-agony is. He felt the terrors of death for Himself; He felt sadness for sin, and fear of hell for us. As His Wounds heal our wounds, so His Agony is the remedy for our last agony. How shall this remedy be applied to our dying brethren? It must be by our prayers and by our supplications.

CHAPTER VIII.

LET US NOT FORSAKE THE DYING.

In former times every Christian prepared for death. Works on this subject. But now the dying often will not even see a Priest. Touching prayer of a dying Religious, that the dying may not be forsaken. Let us be their visible angels.

IN any society where faith exists, final impenitence is rare. Formerly, every Christian, as he felt death approaching, sought to make his peace with God. There was little need to urge his relations and friends to take measures for his conversion, and to send for a Priest. Many pious works were written with a view of assisting the Faithful in their preparation for a holy death. More than sixty books of this kind have been published, either written in French, or else translated into that language. But in these days of carelessness and irreligion, dying sinners do not think of being converted on their death-bed, they often forbid any one to mention the subject of religion, they will not allow a Priest to come near them, and their families very often have the same opinions as themselves. They do all that can be done for the body, but they have no care for the soul, whose existence and nature is a problem to them, while its eternal destiny is a matter of little moment. We shall soon want books to teach fervent and Apostolic souls how to make their way to the dying, to prepare their minds to believe in God and in His Son Jesus Christ; and, at all events, if they dare not see a Priest or receive the sacraments, may in their last hour hold the symbol of their salvation to their dying lips. Our Saviour, by means of the Devotion to His Agonising Heart, seems to say to the Faithful of our days: " Do not forsake the dying. Strive and pray, use all your efforts to make sure of their conversion and their final perseverance. Even if they have faith and piety they will be beset by temptations which you may lessen for them."

A Religious of the Society of Jesus made a striking appeal to his friends, which will not be out of place here. He had had an apoplectic seizure, the danger had unexpectedly lessened, but he was in a state of great languor and weakness, and expected a return of the attack. He spent his time in meditation on the account given in the Gospels of the death of our Lord. We quote the words which he addressed to his friends, " I pray you by the mercies of Jesus Christ, by your own eternal salvation, and that of the souls intrusted to you, I pray all who are led by charity or duty, to assist the dying, and never to leave them in their extremity. Physicians of the body may despair of a sick person's life, but the physician of the soul should never despair of a sinner's salvation, for that would be to despair of the infinite mercy of God. Never weary of putting before the dying sinner the immense riches of divine mercy, that he may be led to hope and to love. If he can no longer hear your voice, speak to his eyes, show him the ground of our hope and love, the crucified Saviour. If his sight has failed, make him touch the crucifix, that only anchor of hope and of love. Let no means be untried by your ardent charity at this decisive moment, when eternity is at stake. So will you be true followers and worthy ministers of Jesus Christ, Who loved

His own unto the end. I dwell the more on this subject, because I have often observed with sorrow that people talk in the very room where a person is dying, about worldly affairs, in a way which is hurtful to him if he is still conscious, and which in any case is utterly useless. Or else, after saying some prayers and some pious words, they remain silent, as if they had done everything; or again, they devote their attention to the symptoms of approaching death when there is not a moment to lose, as any moment may decide his state for eternity. I myself, a poor sinner, have been very near that last hour of which I am speaking, and I am likely soon to relapse into it, without any hope of further recovery. I am dying daily; this indeed is the common lot of man, for our life diminishes as it grows longer. But my peculiar lot is to see and feel that I am really dying daily, *quotidie morior* (1 Cor. xv. 31); my courage fails me, my senses are dimmed, my mind wanders, my limbs totter, I am bowed down, and I crave for support—*Miseremini amici mei* (Job xix. 21). Therefore, while I am still able, I beseech my faithful friends, that when the time comes that I shall be in the greatest need, and yet unable to ask for help, they will not fail me—*Miseremini mei, saltem vos amici mei!* I beseech them, I say, by the love of Jesus Christ, by everything that can touch true and loving and beloved hearts, that they will not leave me alone, but will constantly suggest to me those sentiments of faith, hope, and love in which I wish to live and die. Even if I should have a very long and violent last agony, like some whom I have witnessed, oh, my friends! in charity do not forsake me. What are four-and-twenty hours more of trouble and care to you in comparison with a happy or a miserable eternity to your dying friend? It is the last and greatest mark of affection that I ask for, and I shall be grateful to you through all eternity in that place of rest which I hope to reach through the mercy of our Saviour. A true friend never forsakes one, and especially in affliction and at the hour of death."*

Let us then be faithful to our friends and relations in their death agony. "Do not abandon me," is their cry. "You have solaced me in my lifetime with your love, and your care, and your counsels; be with me at the hour of my departure, assist me with good and holy words, with prayers and supplications, and make intercession for me to the Sovereign Judge Who is to pronounce my eternal sentence."

The Guardian Angels of the dying speak for them; they seem to say to us—"Though we do not share the same nature, we have never forsaken a human being committed to our care. Day and night for twenty, for fifty years, our solicitude has been unceasing. Shall such devo-

* Tubolet, *Reflexions sur J. C. mourant*, ch. xviii.

tion become useless by your fault? Will you refuse to cooperate with us for the salvation of this soul? Oh, no; surely you will be, as far as in you lies, guardians and visible angels of the dying."

CHAPTER IX.

REASONS FOR HASTE.

Reasons of our prayers for the dying. Jesus asks it of us. We pay homage to His Agony when we trust them to His Agonising Heart. Time presses. Let our assistance be in proportion to the necessity for it. Let us be apostles. Let us pray by working and by suffering. We shall be prayed for in our turn.

By prayer for the dying we give glory to Jesus Christ, we do great good to our neighbour, we gain the most precious benefits for ourselves. By prayer for the dying we offer the best and sweetest consolation to the heart of Jesus, for we save the souls for whom He suffered. By prayer for the dying we fulfil a most Catholic Apostolate, one which is, in the fullest sense of the word, universal, for death spares no man— one which is most necessary, since a good death is its object, and most urgent, for all eternity may depend on this moment. More than eighty thousand souls are to appear this day before the tribunal of God. How many, alas! will be overtaken in their sins? How many others will be harassed by temptations of the devil, or by fear of their Judge? Pray for them to-day; make haste; to-morrow it will be too late. You pray for the souls in Purgatory, whose happiness is certain though it be delayed, and will you not pray for the poor dying, whose salvation is uncertain—is even in great danger? You pray for the conversion of sinners, though you know that, while life lasts, delay is not irreparable, and will you neglect the dying, who are already on the very threshold of eternity. A day, an hour, a moment more, and it will be Heaven or hell for ever!*

Listen to Jesus Himself, Who pleads the cause of the dying. Hear Him say—"I have tasted the bitterness of all agonies. All those in their last agony are under My protection, their loneliness makes them all the dearer to My Heart. I know what it is to be forsaken. In My Agony on the Cross I complained to My Father that He had forsaken Me, although Mary My Mother, and John My beloved Disciple, stood at My Feet. In My Agony in the Garden of Olives I felt the indifference and the slumber of My Apostles. I said to you through them—'Watch and pray;' watch and pray for those who die each day, watch and pray for those who are suffering and dying at this very moment!"

Happy thought, to place the dying under care

* *Grande Confrérie du Cœur Agonisant à Jérusalem,* No. II.

G

of the suffering Heart of Jesus. Who can sympathise as He does with every agony? Who is better able to help? What does He wait for? One prayer from us. He waits that the breath of our supplications may bring from His Heart a drop of that Blood which was poured forth in the Garden of Gethsemane and on the mountain of Calvary, as a refreshing dew for the sinners who are dying to-day. O Lord, we honour Thy Agony by placing in it all our confidence, by owning that even where Thou seemest weakest Thou art able to save the dying from the abyss, and to open Heaven to them. Oh, Agonising Heart of My God, I will henceforth pay Thee this tribute of love; I will daily intrust the souls of the dying to Thee, that Thou mayest save them; I will bring them to Thee as to a refuge, and I will unite my prayers to all those who pray to Thee for their everlasting salvation.

Time presses; they have but a year, a month, a week, part of a day, to be converted and forgiven. Before the end of the day which has now begun, time for them will be no more; their eternal doom will be decided—Heaven for ever or hell for ever, the eternal joys of the blessed or the eternal fires of the damned! Alas! the flames have even now almost reached them. It is not my neighbour's house that is in danger, but his body, his soul, his whole being. Help! help! Bring the water of prayer, stretch out the arm of charity, and he may still be saved from the devouring fire. Your small efforts may cause his redemption, for they may make the pains, the miracles, the teaching, the Blood, the death of Jesus applicable to the salvation of his soul.

Amongst the eighty thousand who die each day how many are idolaters, sinners, forsaken, without any help save yours? Let your help, then, be equal to their necessity, to their numbers, to their loneliness; measure it out by the depth of hell, which must be closed beneath them, by Heaven, which must be opened above them; measure it out by the temptations which assail them, by the number of demons who lie in wait for them; measure it by the Agonising Heart of your Saviour, Who has given you all without measure. Did He reserve anything when He gave Himself for us? Oh, keep nothing back, give all to Him in the person of the dying!

Do you not know that many generous souls give all to the dead who are detained in the flames of Purgatory? Do you not know what others do to bring sinners back; what our Missionaries do every day for the conversion of the heathen? Yet those in Purgatory have the certainty of endless bliss—their entrance into it is only delayed. The sinners and heathen still on earth, if they are converted to-day may be lost to-morrow. But if you can rescue the agonising from sin and from hell they are safe for ever, their final perseverance is assured, for they are to die to-day. Without leaving your home you become a missionary, a deliverer of souls. The whole world is the field of your apostleship; death is everywhere, and everywhere your prayer can help the dying. It goes further than our ships or armies, further even than the Ministers of the Gospel. They cannot be in all places, they cannot be with all the dying. But as the influence of the Heart of Jesus is omnipresent, the prayer you make to Him for the dying may have universal influence.

Pray not only with your lips and your heart, pray by your good works, by patience in your sufferings. Offer to God your labours, your trials, your afflictions, your daily life, for those who die each day, and you have nothing to envy the Missionary save his fatigues and his generous toils. You, like him, have whole nations to evangelise; you may be missionaries for Japan, for Tonkin, for China, for the inhospitable shores of Africa and Oceanica, for the wandering tribes of America, yea, even for all countries. The only limits to your zeal are the limits of the world.

Give all, and you shall have it given back to you at the hour of your own death. Others will pray for you, as you have prayed for others. The Blessed Virgin will assist you as she assisted her only Son. Jesus will make you know the wondrous virtue of His Agony, and all the dying whom you have delivered will unite their voices before the Throne of God to gain all His mercy for you. Say to Him in the depths of your heart—"O my dear Saviour! I behold Thee in the poor, I receive Thee in the stranger, I visit Thee in the sick, all that I do for the least of Thy brethren I do for Thy sake. I wish to see Thee, to love Thee, and to succour Thee also in the dying. Thou suffering Heart of Jesus, I wish to console Thee in all suffering hearts! O Heart of the Divine Spouse of our souls! Thou art the aim of my ambition ; I aspire to Thee, all my efforts and prayers are that I may possess Thee. Oh, then, give Thyself to me now, at the hour of my death and for ever, in return for what I give the dying each day!"

II.—THE CONFRATERNITY.

CHAPTER I.

OLD ASSOCIATIONS FOR THE RELIEF OF THE DYING.

Influence of the Association. The holy women on Calvary. The service of the hospitals, and of the ministers of the sick. Confraternity of the Holy Agony of our Lord. Bona Mors under the protection of the holy Angels. Confraternity of St. Francis of Sales for the agonising.

IN the order of grace, as well as in the order of nature, union is strength; union gives us power over the Heart of God as well as over the hearts of men. Our Lord Himself has said, "If two of you shall consent upon earth concerning anything whatsoever they shall ask, it shall be done to them by My Father Who is in Heaven. For where there are two or three gathered together in My name, there am I in the midst of them" (Matt. xviii. 19, 20). Therefore, in all ages of the Church, Associations have been among the principal means employed for the salvation of the dying.

A pious author traces their origin to those holy women who by their prayers contributed to the salvation of the good thief, and assisted the Saviour while He was dying on the Cross (John xix. 25). " Here," he says " we have the pattern of the pious Associations established in the Church for the succour and consolation of the Faithful in their agony. As Jesus bore our sorrows, and was Himself their remedy, He was pleased not only to suffer all that is most terrible in the agony of death, but also to instruct His followers how they were to help each other in that last struggle. For this purpose, He who was the strength of the Angels, let them come down from Heaven to console and strengthen Him. For this purpose, the daughters of Jerusalem were led to meet together, and bear Him company, showing their compassion and gratitude on Mount Calvary. Their charity led them to assemble in the earthly Jerusalem from different parts of Judea, and made them resolve to go with Jesus at any cost to the place of His suffering, and not to forsake Him in death. Christians, who are led by the same spirit to take part in Associations for the succour of the dying, never forget that Jesus has approved of your holy Assemblies in the persons of the daughters of Jerusalem; that He has by Himself sanctified your care for sinners in their agony, and that He is in a special manner present with those who pray for the dying."*

* Tribolet, *Reflexions sur J. C. mourant*, ch. viii.

The desire for the salvation of the dying was the origin of those charitable Associations by which our hospitals have been brought to their present state of perfection.

The first hospital was founded in Rome, in the days of St. Jerome, by an illustrious penitent named Fabiola, who herself undertook the most servile offices for the sake of the sick.* But as time went on, hospitals were left to the care of hirelings, who did not imitate the devotion of the Saint. These abodes of suffering were held in such horror, that fear of their lives often deterred even Priests of moderate learning from carrying the consolations of religion to the sick and dying. In times of pestilence and contagious disease, no one could be found to fulfil these offices save Priests who, as penance for some crime, were condemned by their Bishops to live in the hospitals. Cicatelli, a disciple of St. Camillus of Lellis, gives details too dreadful to repeat. The hired Ministers, he tells us, gave but scanty care to the bodies of the sick, and what they did was done without kindness or skill. The sufferers sometimes passed whole days without the necessary remedies, sometimes they were ill-treated, and made the sport of the wretched mercenaries even in their last moments. Their beds were made so seldom, that they were full of vermin and filth. Before

* St. Jerome, *Epist.* lxxxiv. *ad Oceanum,* t. iv., p. 660. Edit. Bened.

the dying had breathed their last, they were either just left where they lay, and covered with a sheet, or carried away, thrown amongst corpses, or buried alive. Even at Rome, the capital of charity, this happened several times in the course of a few years. When these miserable beings recovered their consciousness, and realised their horrible position, they died of terror, or went mad. One of them, however, survived for several years; he was known to our author, who makes this reflection on the dark picture he has presented to us: " If such things were possible in Rome, the mirror of the Christian world, the head-quarters of holiness and charity, what must have been the state of other towns which were without the presence and care of the Sovereign Pontiff and so many zealous ecclesiastics? These crying needs decided St. Camillus to found the Religious Order of Ministers of the Sick. He knew by experience that many conversions might be made among the sick and the dying in the hospitals, and he said to his disciples, 'My Fathers and Brethren, what better Indies or Japan need our Congregation desire in order to convert souls to the Lord than these holy hospitals.'"*

Many other Religious Orders for the relief of the sick and dying have arisen since those days,

* Cicatelli, *Vita del V. P. Camillo de Lellis*, l. ii., ch. i.

and their zeal for the soul has taught them to bestow the tenderest care on the body. Even among seculars many Confraternities have been established, with a holy death as their object. In 1648, Father Vincent Caraffa, General of the Society of Jesus, conceived the idea of founding at Rome the Association of the Holy Agony of our Lord Jesus Christ dying on Calvary, and of Our Lady of Dolours. This Confraternity is commonly known by the name of the Bona Mors, because all its members seek that grace for themselves by honouring the holy Agony of our dying Saviour, and the sorrowful martyrdom which His Blessed Mother suffered at the foot of the Cross. Pope Innocent X. sanctioned the formation of the Confraternity, the blessing of God evidently went with it, and it has spread throughout the Christian world.* On the 18th of April, 1809, Pius VII., in order to encourage the Faithful to pray for the dying, granted an indulgence of three hundred days to all who say three *Paters* and three *Aves* for them, in memory of the Agony of Jesus and the sorrows of Mary on Mount Calvary, and a plenary indulgence to those who say these prayers every day for a month.†

The most holy Virgin, assisting her Divine

* *Exercice pour se préparer à la mort* p. 3, 4. St. Malo, 1787.
† *Manuel Le Chrétien éclairé sur le nature et l'usage des Indulgences*, 8e edit., p. 11, art. i., n. 37.

Son in His Agony, has been often invoked on behalf of the dying. In the church of Saint Pierre de Mortagne there was a Confraternity of Our Lady of the Agonising. The Bishop of Rochelle gave the necessary permission on the 18th of January, 1658; on the 2nd of February it was established, and on the 27th of the same month approved by Alexander VII., who granted indulgences to its members.* Another Confraternity of the same name existed in the parish church of Our Lady of the Assumption, at Villefranche de Lauraguais, in the diocese of Toulouse, and enjoyed similar privileges, conferred on it by the Holy Father. It was transferred in 1800 to the parish church of St. Peter and the branch chapel of Nazareth. The following prayer is used by the Associates: "I honour thee, O holy Virgin at the foot of the Cross, and I most humbly pray thee to be with me in my agony and at my death, as thou wast with thy beloved Son. I venerate thee, O Mother of my God, because thou hast power to dispense the Precious Blood of thy dear Son, and I beseech thee by thy divine maternity to apply Its merits to me at the hour of my death, and to offer to the Eternal Father all the sufferings of thy dear Son, His humiliations, and His adorable death, to satisfy His divine justice, instead of that eternal death

* *Pour la Confrérie de Notre Dame des Agonisants*, petit. in 32. Fontenay, 1658.

and those sufferings which I have merited for my sins."*

The holy Angels have also been invoked for a good death, and Father Coret, a Jesuit, published a book called *The Association, or Good Death under the Patronage of the holy Guardian Angels*. He brings forward a great many examples of the assistance given by these heavenly spirits at the hour of death to those who had thought of them devoutly through their lives. "I have seen," he tells us, "on their death-beds many who have loved their good Angels, and I have always been struck by their great joy. They have said—'O God, how glad I am that I have loved and invoked my Guardian Angel;' 'I never thought I should die so happy;' 'Blessed Angel, this is the moment of my need, and you have not failed me.' Prelates, even as they were about to die, have exclaimed — 'Who would have thought that death, which seems dreadful afar off, could be so easy when it comes near to us! It is by your aid, blessed Angel, friend of my soul!' Do not believe in this especial Angelic aid merely on my word, or even on that of St. Onuphrius, who relates how his Guardian Angel, having led him to the desert, went away, saying: 'Serve God well during your life, and leave

---

* *Exercice de Dévotion pour les personnes Associées à la Confrérie de Notre Dame des Agonisants*, petit. in 32, p. 57. Toulouse, 1802.

your death to me.' But take our Lord's own words in the Gospel. He tells us how the Angels attended the dying Lazarus, and carried him to Abraham's bosom, giving us the hope that they will perform the same good offices for us."*

The Faithful have also sought the grace of a good death by the intercession of different Saints. A Confraternity of St. Francis of Sales for the dying was established at the parish church of St. Louis, in Paris, by authority of the Archbishop, on the 19th of January, 1680. Innocent XI. confirmed it, and enriched it with indulgences on the 26th of March in the same year.† There are many devotions and prayers addressed to St. Joseph, to obtain the grace of dying as he did in the arms of Jesus and Mary.

* Coret, *l'Association*, 4e edit., ch. i., n. 2. Rennes, 1742.
† *Institution de la Confrérie de Saint François de Sales pour les Agonisants*, nouvelle edit. Paris, 1713, in 12.

CHAPTER II.

THE NEW ASSOCIATION SUITED TO THE PRESENT TIME.

Fitness of devotion to the Agonising Heart, as regards its object of veneration and its object of supplication. Prayer is often our only way of promoting the salvation of the dying. The association of the " Solidaires " and its motto. Episcopal condemnation. Support from Freemasonry. Opposition to this satanic society becomes a necessity. Mission of the Associates of the Agonising Heart. An ingenious method adopted.

THERE is an admirable fitness in the great works of the Spirit of God for the good of mankind which cannot fail to strike us and to rejoice our hearts. We see it in the object of veneration and the object of supplication brought before us by the Devotion to the suffering Heart of Jesus.

This Divine Heart was pleased to manifest Itself especially to the world in the midst of the revolutions and troubles, which marked the middle of the present century with tears and blood. Long-established Powers were tottering from their foundations; their downfal threatened to involve the ruin of public and private fortunes; the Sovereign Pontiff, the common Father of the Faithful and the Vicar of Jesus Christ, was in sorrowful and bitter exile, and even when he returned to his capital his grievous suffering was not at an end. Indifference, rationalism, and impiety, were inventing new means of frustrating the grace and mercy of God, of setting Him at naught in His word and His laws, of wounding the Heart of His Son, and of multiplying His sorrows and agonies. At the sight of these miseries a sort of agony overwhelmed the hearts of the most faithful and devoted followers of the Saviour; they suffered with their good Master, they longed to satisfy the justice of God. How eager they were to honour the holy Agony of Jesus! How happy to gather round His Agonising Heart, as round a centre of warmth and of life which might still restore vitality to the fainting body of society! Devotion to the Agonising Heart of Jesus comes before us as a remedy for sin, a support for the wretched, a consolation for all. It raises a banner of hope round which Christendom may still rally.

But even more manifestly is it fitted to succour and save the dying. Doubtless the passage from time to eternity has ever been beset with perils, and spiritual help for the dying has never been out of season. But formerly it was easier to give it. When people were, during life, less unfaithful to their religious duties, they did not shrink from receiving a Minister of God in their last hours. Now, minds are but little enlightened by supernatural faith, hearts are not warmed with love of Jesus Christ, the laws of His Church are neglected by many men, and even women, who have no care save for their material interests, who listen only to bad doctrines, who frequent only infidel or impious society, who live far from God, and who do not attempt to obey His Gospel, or even to think of eternity. When sinners like these are laid on a bed of suffering, when death is knocking at their very door, when their eternal doom is about to be pronounced, those who might do something for their salvation are kept at a distance. Their own prejudices and the prejudices of their families bar the door against any one distinguished by a Religious dress or known to profess a particular form of religion. Or perhaps the Minister of reconciliation is sent for merely that one who is dead, or has already lost the use of his reason, may not be refused Christian burial.

What is left for Christian charity to do? Since so many of the dying cannot be reached by its special representatives, it endeavours to reach them by the breath of prayer. The souls which are about to pass from earth to God's tribunal are like the flocks of birds which sometimes light on the ground, awaiting a favourable wind to pursue their way. The wings of the soul are good desires. Who will give wings to the sinner's soul? who will give him holy desires, that he may rise from earth like the dove and soar to the eternal tabernacles? The charity of fervent souls who are praying and suffering and working for the dying will avail to do this. That charity will gain conversion for the sinner, will persuade him to receive the sacraments of the Church, or to make an act of perfect contrition before he leaves this world. This result will be obtained more rarely for those who are strangers to the faith, for Jews, Mussulmen, and idolaters. But who, that believes the teaching of the Holy Scriptures as to the efficacy of prayer, can doubt that the daily supplications of souls devoted to the suffering Heart of our Saviour are answered by innumerable graces of conversion and salvation, of perseverance and perfection, bestowed on the Faithful who are dying every day? In the eighteenth century, while the friends of the Heart of Jesus were saddened by many fearful deaths, books of preparation, suited for the use of every one, abounded. Blessed be God, Who in these our days, when most men think little of preparing themselves for death, has raised up a fervent Association to pray for those who will not pray for themselves, to strive to save those who are bent on their own destruction, and to awaken faith and charity in hearts that have long been careless and forgetful!

The very character of our Association gives a special fitness to this effort now that societies have made it their object to prevent all preparation for death. The spirit of "association" is rife in our days; men bind themselves together to die in impenitence and impiety. Belgium offers a sad example. Some people in that country have formed themselves into a body, which undertakes to refuse any minister of religion access to its dying members, and to have its dead buried with uproar and impiety. Their motto is—"No Priest at births, or marriages, or deaths."*

At the beginning of the year 1863, Mgr. Malou, Bishop of Bruges, condemned these associations in the following terms:—

"Freemasonry, by the mouth of its grave authorities and its young adepts, has hurled a defiance and an anathema at the religion of Christ, and that from the open grave of its brethren who have died enemies of Jesus Christ. This society gives us to understand that those who enrol themselves in its ranks are bound to it for life and death; it watches their death-beds to hold them to their apostacy, and to keep out the Priest and the Cross, penitence and hope. Be it known, therefore, that the anathemas of the Church have not lost their power; and that these fearful impenitent deaths, which make every Catholic heart tremble, justify their severity. This last sect, the Freemasonry of 'Solidaires,' or 'freed men,' &c., has been lately established in the capital and in most of the great towns. It is chiefly composed of men and women of the lower orders, who in return for the honour of belonging to a sect of free-thinkers, and for

* *Le Monde*, numero du Lundi, 25 Juillet, 1864.

the advantage of assistance during illness and a gratuitous civil funeral, engage themselves to abandon the Church through life, and to refuse the sacraments at their death; to imitate the conduct and the end of their chiefs and instructors—that is to say, to live atheists and die reprobates. What an odious part do these false apostles of reason, liberty, and human dignity assume, who, taking advantage of the frailty of the heart and the weakness of the understanding, pervert men's souls, rob them of their faith, and give them in its stead not a new belief, not assertions, not even doubts—but blasphemies; who work upon misery and vice to gain disciples to apostacy, who tyrannise over the conquered by interest and human respect, who pursue their victim to his very death-bed, who keep watch over his agony that they may check the prayer that would rise from his lips and stifle the first movements of repentance in his heart! Oh, if it be 'a fearful thing to fall into the hands of the living God' Whom we have despised, what is the crime of those who fling the slaves of their fanaticism at the very feet of the Sovereign Judge?"*

About the middle of the year 1865, the society of Freemasons expressed its sympathy with the dreadful sect of the "Solidaires," to which it had already given many members. In England, France, and Italy, Freemasons rejoiced

* *Le Monde*, Vendredi, 6 Mars, 1863.

in the formation of associations where men pledged themselves to die without God, like brute beasts. The London Freemasons wrote—"We have learnt with pleasure that the free-thinkers of Belgium have succeeded in organising companies for civil funerals. We sincerely congratulate our Belgian brethren on this happy idea, and especially the Freemasons who have been so ready to take the initiative in this rationalistic movement. A great example has been given to the world, and we doubt not that it will bear fruit. Much has been done already, by taking so large a proportion of the dead from the Church; but the work is only beginning—to complete it, we must also rescue the living from the power of the Priests."*

Encouraged by such support, the "Solidaires" are spreading throughout Europe. In Paris they sometimes form a barrier round a death-bed, lest the Priest should come and the soul be saved.

Ought not this satanic union to be met by an angelic association? Ought not the friends of God to be as full of energy as the instruments of Satan? Will they give up the field to this infernal zeal? Since union is strength, must they not bind themselves together to stem this torrent of pride and impiety? Does not this new evil call for a special and vigorous remedy? If we only do what we have done already, if we content ourselves with obtaining a good death

* *Le Monde*, Samedi, 16 Septembre, 1865.

for ourselves and other members of pious Confraternities, would not our consciences reproach us with indolence and cowardice in face of our foes? They spare no efforts, they shrink from no sacrifices, to ruin the souls of the dying. And shall we, the disciples or ministers of Jesus Christ, be lukewarm and indifferent in His cause? Shall we draw back at some little difficulty, shall we prove unequal to acts of self-abnegation and of generosity, when it may be in our power to rescue souls that are on the very brink of hell? Oh, surely the very name of Agony would be our condemnation, for agony means struggle and combat. What struggles, what combats has the Heart of Jesus encountered for our salvation! Ought not our grateful hearts to enter upon them readily, to suffer to the utmost in order to help forward the salvation of our dying brethren?

What a mission lies before the Association of the Agonising Heart of Jesus for those who die each day! If we can gain access to their bed of suffering, we speak to them of Christ and bring them back to God! At least, we fall on our knees many times a day to pray that God will shower down blessings and graces on the dying. There are rocky deserts and burning sands, watered by no stream, and which the skill of man cannot irrigate, but God sends clouds laden with rain to refresh them, that they may not be altogether barren; so hardened souls, withered and scorched by vice, are reached by our prayers, which, like a cloud, rise above all barriers and overcome all obstacles to bear to them the grace of penitence and conversion.

A fervent layman who was in the habit of visiting the Hôtel Dieu at Lyons, used to make out each month a list of those who were most dangerously ill, indicating them merely by their number, and adding a few words as to their moral state and to commend them to the prayers of devout Christians. God blessed the effort, and those who had prayed soon rejoiced over conversions obtained by their supplications. What an encouragement for all members of the Confraternity of the Agonising Heart of Jesus! What a certain and easy mode of doing battle with the legions of hell! O Sacred and loving Heart! bless Thy friends and servants more and more abundantly, that they may lead those souls into the way of truth whom Thine enemies are seeking to draw downwards to perdition!

CHAPTER III.
PROGRESS OF THE WORK.

Short prayer to the Agonising Heart distributed everywhere, like a blessed seed. Benevolent assistance of pious persons. Association established at Bourges, at Mans, at Niort, and Limoges. Interior progress of the work, or greater perfection of means. How the Association may be established.

WE may sometimes have seen a flower which has been transplanted by the hand of man to a distance from its native soil, blooming alone, but after it has come to perfection, the wind bears its seeds away, and by-and-bye they spring up and adorn the hills and valleys around. The Devotion to the Agonising Heart of Jesus, after lying hid for a long time in the breast of a humble Religious, blossomed forth in a short and touching prayer. "But," says the *Messenger of the Sacred Heart*, "how is this little germ to increase and bear fruit? What mysterious gale is to bear it to the east and to the west, and in a few years make it spread to the most distant lands? It is the word of Christ's Vicar, enriching it with precious indulgences. With the blessing of the Holy Father, it has gone forth in all directions, and translations in different languages have made it familiar in most Catholic countries."*

* *Le Messager du Sacré Cœur.* Novembre, 1861, art. i., n. iii., p. 186.

Devotion to the Agonising Heart has been very widely propagated by means of little books translated into several of the European languages, and even into Hindostanee. It appeared most opportunely on the eve of those sad events which were to imperil so many souls; it took root in countries which were about to become the theatre of bloody warfare, and where the number of the dying was to be multiplied by the sword. It reached Upper Italy, Sicily, Naples, North America, and even Poland. May we not hope that the Agonising Heart of our good Master, touched by so many prayers, wrought wonderful works of mercy on the great fields of death?

The cooperation of pious persons was not wanting. We have already mentioned several names, and will now add others. Father de Busse, of revered memory, distributed many tickets for our Devotion during his Missions; Mgr. Foulquier permitted the insertion of the prayer, "O most merciful Jésus" in the book of prayers which he caused to be printed for the use of his diocese. In the diocese of Mende, the children in the different educational institutions are taught to repeat it, and it is said on Sundays in many churches at the Mass in which the sermon is preached. The Rev. Father Studer, Provincial of Toulouse, showed a paternal affection for this work, and especially for the Community. The Rev. Father Beckx, the

General of the Society of Jesus, inherited the benevolence of his predecessor. Father Pellico, brother of the celebrated author, took a particular interest in this Devotion. Father de Villefort, the friend of the French in Rome, employed one of the best artists of that capital to paint a picture of the Agonising Heart of Jesus, which may be copied for the Confraternities. Laymen have also shown great zeal in propagating this Devotion, and a worthy Christian mayor of a commune near Paris has made himself an apostle of the Agonising Heart. The progress of the Association has kept pace with the progress of the Devotion. Holy Priests have advocated it warmly, and the Faithful have responded eagerly. Confraternities have been erected, with the approbation of the Bishops, in many towns of France, and considerable good has been done by them to their Associates, as well as to the dying. The Association established at Bourges, in the church of the Jesuit Fathers, numbered, in 1861, six thousand members, many of whom take it in turns to go to Holy Communion, and make half an hour's intercession daily for the dying. Many offer an annual alms to have Masses said for them. At Mans, the Confraternity was erected by Mgr. Nanquette, and approved on the 20th of September, 1859, by the Sovereign Pontiff, who granted indulgences in its favour. Each member contributes to the frequent cele-

I

bration of the Holy Sacrifice for the dying by an annual gift of a franc.* At Niort, the Association, established in connection with the Church of St. Andrew in 1863, has eight or nine hundred members. The Nuns of St. Alexis, at Limoges, who serve the hospital of the town, established the Association there, and their new church was consecrated by Mgr. Fruchaud, under the patronage of the Agonising Heart of Jesus. We shall speak at length, and in a separate chapter, of the Archconfraternity at Jerusalem.

Any work really inspired by the Spirit of God is sure to grow, not only externally, but, above all, internally, and the growth will be both in height and in depth. It is like a germ which as it expands not only becomes larger, but is more perfect in every part. This double progress of grace is seen in the work of the Agonising Heart; it has gained at once in extension and in organisation. Its fundamental practice is perpetual intercession made by the Associates in turn. It is made, if possible, from half-past two to three o'clock, in honour of our Saviour's dying Agony on the Cross. Each Associate takes one day in the month, and the short prayer we have already quoted is said daily by all. If one day in the month can be chosen, a Friday for example, for intercession

* Boulangé, *Manuel de la Confrérie du Cœur Agonisant*, p. 28—31. Le Mars, 1860, in 32.

in common, the work is regularly established. This is the centre of all the other exercises. It is desirable to have a chapel, or at least some special place where the intercession may be made, and to have there a little picture of the Agonising Heart; for devotion is aided by some object which appeals to the senses. An intelligent and pious directress should take charge of the whole, assigning to each person a day for intercession, and taking care to see that it is faithfully performed.

Other practices may be added: giving alms for Masses for the dying, Communion made by each Associate on a certain day in the month, visits to the dying and the sick, especially to those who are dangerously ill. The statutes which have been published by the Founder* provide for all these things; and in many places the whole system is working with the best results.

All these things may be done as matters of private devotion, without any sanction of ecclesiastical authority; but it is to be wished that Confraternities should be duly established, meeting every month for an instruction and Benediction, and for this establishment episcopal approbation is necessary. When constituted, they can be affiliated to the Archconfraternity

* R. P. Lyonnard, *Le Cœur Agonisant de Jésus et les Agonisants de chaque jour*, p. 57, et suiv. Paris, 1864, in 32°.

at Jerusalem, and share in its indulgences. Pious people often wish to set the thing going in their parish, but do not know how to begin. If thirty people, men or women, can be found to undertake the half hour's intercession each once a month, the Association may be provisionally established. If it perseveres, the authorisation of the Bishop will give it a canonical form, and other practices can be added at discretion.

When an individual wishes to belong to the Association, it is only necessary that the name be sent to the Superior of the Nuns of the Agonising Heart.*

CHAPTER IV.

VISITING THE SICK.

Recommended by the Founder. The first Confraternity of Charity and the society of ladies established by St. Vincent of Paul for the purpose of visiting the sick. Much good is still done in Paris by this society. The Association of the Agonising Heart promotes the same work. Statutes relative to visiting the sick. How God leads founders and developes their undertakings.

THE interior progress of the work of the Agonising Heart is one which has regard to persons and to acts. As to persons, some generous souls have been led to devote them-

* A Lyon, Quartier de Monplaisir, aux Quatre-Maisons, 11.

selves by vows as a complete sacrifice to God, in order to obtain salvation for the dying. The third section of this book gives a detailed account of this Religious Community. The practice of visiting the sick and dying, with a view of preparing the way for their conversion, has been added to the daily prayer and constant attendance at Mass. The pious Founder of the Confraternity says:—"For the better attainment of the object in view, members will, as far as possible, add *performance* to *prayer*. They will gladly visit and console the sick, they will exhort them to offer up their sufferings to God, and, above all, to receive the last sacraments. These offices of charity should be performed for the dying of all classes, but most especially for hardened sinners, for the poor and desolate, and for any who may be exposed, by the negligence of those around them, to the danger of dying without receiving the sacraments."*

The first charitable Confraternity for visiting the sick poor was founded at Châtillon in 1617, by St. Vincent de Paul.† In 1629 he established another in Paris, where its success was marvellous.‡ In 1634 he founded a society of ladies, to visit the sick in the hospitals of the capital. His biographer, Abelly, says:—"God only knows all the good that has thus been

---

* *Le Cœur Agonisant Statuts*, art. v.
† Abelly, *Vie de St. Vincent de Paul*, l. i., ch. xiii.
‡ *Ibid.*, ch. xxix.

done with the help of His grace; He only knows how many have been led to die a happy death or to begin a holy life. If, however, we may judge by the number of religious conversions which have taken place, we may fairly infer that many have been rescued from a life of immorality. For even in the first year, God so abundantly blessed this work that more than seven hundred and sixty persons submitted to the Church. Among them were Lutherans, Calvinists, and Turks. Many of them had been wounded and taken prisoners at sea, and sent to the Hôtel Dieu. Vincent spoke one day to the ladies, of the gratitude they ought to show to God, Who had been pleased to choose them and make use of them to bring about so much good. 'Ladies,' said he, 'you ought to thank God very much for having led you to take such care of the bodily wants of the poor, for while tending their bodies His grace has made you also think of the salvation of their souls, and this at the most fitting time, for the greater number of them have no other seasonable moment to prepare themselves properly for their last hour. And even those who have recovered might never have thought of changing their present lives, had it not been for the good influences which have been brought to bear upon them.'"* The Saints have a power of giving life and permanence to the works they

* Abelly, *Vie de St. Vincent de Paul*, l. ii., ch. iv.

originate; the Church weathers all storms, and institutions which are really useful to her share her stability. The society of ladies founded by St. Vincent de Paul still exists in Paris; it comprises visitors, assistants, and collectors. The account of its operations in a single year, taken at random from its statistics, may give an idea of what has been done in two centuries. In 1863, twelve hospitals, containing 2,560 beds in the women's wards, were regularly visited; 273 convalescent girls were placed in the Asylum of the Sacred Heart of Mary; 420 convalescent children were received in the Asylum of the Infant Jesus, where 120 first Communions were received; 1,490 poor sick families were visited and assisted; 67 couples were married; 60 children were apprenticed, and 131 taken under protection. A great many conversions took place, especially among the dying.

Such is the admirable work in which the Associates of the Agonising Heart of Jesus cooperate, at once enlarging its sphere and giving a fresh impulse to its efforts. It will now no longer be confined to a society of ladies in Paris; but in the country as well as in towns, in other lands as well as in France, Associations of men as well as of women will be formed and organised, for the purpose of visiting the sick and showing the way of salvation to the dying. A great warfare will be waged against the spirit of evil, certain victory will be gained over the "Solidaires," and a multitude of souls will undoubtedly be won over to Christ. We proceed to give some extracts from the statutes, which were approved by the Bishop of Mende, Nov. 6, 1863.

"The visitors are chosen from amongst the Associates, who voluntarily present themselves to undertake the office. The important duties which it entails ought only to be intrusted to persons of known prudence and charity, with some experience, and, if possible, a position and character which may ensure their influence with the sick. Their chief work is to go to the sick, especially to those who are in danger, to encourage them, to urge them to receive the last sacraments, and to help them in preparing for a happy death. The visitors should inform the Priest when the case seems serious, particularly if the friends of the sick person are not likely to do so. All the sick, without distinction of rank, are recommended to the care of the visitors, but the preference should be given to hardened sinners, to the poor and lonely, and to members of the Association. Visitors will inform the president or vice-president when the sick are in need, and on presenting a signed authorisation to the treasurer they will receive adequate help, the authorisation being retained by the treasurer. They will tell the director, or one of the so-called 'zelateurs,' of those who are in danger of death, that the prayers of the Association may be asked for them, above all for those whose spiritual necessities are greatest. The director will assign to each visitor a certain locality, whose sick are to be regularly visited. If he should be unable to gain admission he will let the president or director know. Visitors should often consider the importance of their work, and the blessings which they may gain for the dying by its faithful performance. And if they sometimes meet with difficulties, let them take courage from the hope of the great rewards which the most generous Heart of Jesus has in store for them at the moment of death and throughout all eternity."*

But this apostolical office, inspired by the suffering Heart of our Divine Master, does not stop here. The Confraternity of Charity, established in some villages in 1617, led, in 1633, to the permanent institution of the Sisters of Charity, whose indefatigable devotedness is known all over the world. The good Bishop of Rodez observes with regard to this Institution : "If it be true, according to the words of the Prophet, that 'Deep calleth unto deep,' it is even more true that one blessing produces another blessing, and that charity, which is the most fruitful of virtues, when it has completed one work begins a second. The Sisters of Charity followed the Confraternity of Charity,

* *Le Cœur Agonisant Statuts*, p. 81—84.

and after God had made Vincent the Founder of a Congregation of men for the evangelisation of the poor, He made him also the Father of a Community of women devoted to the same poor, and especially to those who were sick among them. This work is evidently due to the guidance of Divine Providence, for Vincent did not undertake it entirely of his own accord, but was almost compelled to do so."* God Himself inspires all founders; He gives them, when they look not for it, the first inspiration for their work, He follows it by further inspiration till His design is completed. No one can say what this work of the Agonising Heart of Jesus may, under the gradual and constant influence of His holy inspirations, hereafter become. Its Founder's idea is a unity of prayer and action, and we cannot be wrong in looking forward to a glorious development.

* Abelly, *Vie de St. Vincent de Paul*, l. ii., ch. ii.

CHAPTER V.

PRAYER AND ACTION.

Variety in unity. Contemplative and active Nuns. Apostolic Society of the Sacred Heart. Prayer is the soul of the Society. And action combined with prayer and suffering is its ordinary means.

LET us unite in prayer and action. The work of the Agonising Heart is to cooperate with the general movement directed by the Spirit of God. The works of God are marked by variety in unity, and the Devotion to the Agonising Heart of Jesus bears the same stamp. The object of our veneration is one, the graces we expect to gain from It are many. We look for consolation of all who are in sorrow, whatever may be the length of life before them, we look more especially for salvation for all the dying; they are generally the most afflicted of mankind, because of their sufferings, or because of their unwillingness to leave this world, or because of their apprehension of troubles to come upon their families. To attain our main object, the salvation of the dying, the means which we employ are various. By our prayers, by our homage to the Saviour's Agony, by the consolations we offer Him, by our faithfulness in sharing His sorrows, we seek to ascend to His very Heart; and we return thence with our hands full of graces, our hearts full of compassion, to sweeten the last moments of the dying, to save their souls, and bind them to God for all eternity.

All the Associates take part in this double movement of ascending and descending, but we see its fullest efficacy in those who are entirely consecrated to God, under the protection of the Agonising Heart. Cloistered Nuns ascend the heights of contemplation, that they may follow the Divine Lamb in His Agony in the Garden of Olives, and draw fresh graces for the dying from His Heart. Nuns not bound by the vow of the cloister will descend to the very depths of society, where misery and indigence are often accompanied by forgetfulness of God and spiritual death.

Zealous Priests enrol themselves under the banner of the Divine Heart; in the Holy Sacrifice of the Mass they ascend to the altar, they draw near to the Saviour; in the exercise of their ministry they descend into the consciences of men, bearing the light of faith and the refining fire of penitence. On the 1st of August, 1861, Mgr. Foulquier approved of a holy union of Priests called the Apostolic Society of the Sacred Heart of Jesus. These Priests engage to say a Mass every year, "in order to ask from God, by the sufferings of the Agonising Heart of Jesus, and by the sorrows of the compassionate Heart of Mary—first, Apostolic success in the exercise of their holy ministry—that is, the salvation and perfection of the souls intrusted to their care; secondly, efficacious graces of conversion for those in their parishes and dioceses who do not practise their religion; thirdly, that Apostolic Priests may be raised up, powerful in deeds and in words, burning with zeal for the glory of God and the salvation of souls."*

As the fowler spreads his snares, so the loving Heart of Jesus spreads the net of His charity to take souls captive and bring them to the bliss of Paradise. Thus, those who are devoted to the mystery of Gethsemane, and the Agony of the God-Man, join together, that they may be united more closely to His Agonising Heart, and may bring dying sinners back to Him. Prayer and work, the contemplative and the active life, agree in the same object, and assist each other in the salvation of the dying. Must not the progress of Devotion to the Agonising Heart produce in the souls of the Faithful that patience, that vigilance and prayer, which the Divine Master asked for His chosen Disciples upon the Mount of Olives?—*Sustinete, vigilate, orate* (Matt. xxvi. 38, 41).

Prayer is the soul, action the body; their union is generally necessary for the propagation of life in the order of grace, just as the union of soul and body is in the order of nature. As

* *Voir sur cette Société une feuille imprimée* in 8vo, imprimée à Mende in 1861.

the soul can live separate from the body, so a life of entire contemplation is possible to Christians, and the Church has always approved those spiritual families whose whole occupation is the praise of God, prayer for the living and the dead, and personal sanctification. But as the body cannot live without the soul, a merely active Religious Order would be like a corpse, and the Church would not approve an Institution whose whole aim was external action apart from prayer and exercises of piety. Priests and laymen who live in the world are bound to spend some time in prayer in their own houses and at the foot of the altar. Does not our Lord bid all Christians—those who are walking in obedience to His commandments, as well as those who follow Him in the narrower path of His more intimate precepts—" Always to pray, and not to faint" (Luke xviii. 1). The more zealous a Christian is for the salvation of souls, the more time will he give to prayer, to retirement, and to contemplation. Who was so zealous and ardent in action as the Apostle of the Indies and of the far East, St. Francis Xavier? Yet he was ever ready for prayer and meditation, even shortening his sleep to prolong his hours of intercourse with God. If poverty or illness hinders your active cooperation in good works, pray often, pray while you suffer, and your prayers and your patience may save the souls of the dying, and bring success to the labours of other Associates.

But if you are able to work, do not content yourself with prayer and suffering, add action to prayer. Protestantism, which admits no visible Church, may logically conclude that prayer is our only means of promoting the salvation of our neighbours, and says that our belief alone saves us; but the Catholic religion teaches us that there is a visible Church, that invisible things come to us by means of those which are visible, that the Priesthood, the Word of God, and the Sacraments, are the ordinary channels of inward grace, the instruments which God is pleased to use for the sanctification of our souls. If St. Teresa, a Carmelite Nun, made many conversions, it was not because she was in a cloister, but because in her cloister she found the means of close union with God, and consequent holiness; besides, it is to be observed that the conversions she obtained were generally aided by those means belonging to an active life. Jesus Christ did not say to men, "Take the Bible and believe what you will," nor did He say to His Apostles, "Stay where you are, and do nothing but pray;" He sent them into all the world, *Euntes ergo docete* (Matt. xxviii. 19), to carry the good tidings to all nations, and make them fruitful by their labours and their lives. As time went on, and fresh needs arose, God raised up active men like St. Dominic,

Gusman, and St. Ignatius Loyola, to combat heresy, and to quicken the faith of Christians. Let those then who have no vocation for a contemplative life, who cannot pray a great deal, but have much natural activity, set to work bravely, using their energy in the service of grace, doing all that is in their power for the conversion of souls. Energy and united action, energy directed by faith, union sanctified by prayer, such is the plan of charity which the Holy Spirit now sets before us in order to check those who are drawing on the edge of the abyss, and to revive religion amongst us. By His holy inspiration, apostolic Congregations, and Congregations for instruction, have been founded, old active Orders have been revived, and new ones established. Future generations will owe them much. But they never forget that action without prayer cannot bear fruit, though prayer without action may. They pray long and ardently, as our Lord prayed in His Agony, God gives them the assistance of those contemplative Communities whom He has restored to us, that the triumph of the militant Orders may be hastened. St. Teresa says: " If we can by our prayers contribute to this victory, we in our solitude shall have done something for the cause of God. No prayers can be better or more profitable than these."* Alas! in the present day people have not faith enough to

* St. Thérèse, *Le chemin de la perfection*, ch. iii.

understand the perfection and importance of the contemplative Orders. We must not, however, suppose that this tone of mind has any influence in determining the nature of the vocation which leads many generous souls to give up all, and sacrifice themselves for the instruction of children or the care of the sick. Vocation is not human, but divine. If a mixed life of action, joined to prayer, attracts more souls in the present day than a life of complete contemplation, the reason is to be found in the will of God, and in our wretched condition. To attribute it to caprice, to nature, prejudice, or fashion, would be a blasphemy against Providence, which calls together many workmen to raise the temple from its ruins, inspires them with courage to labour with one hand while they fight with the other, and teaches them how to mould the living souls for that spiritual edifice.

The Institution of the Agonising Heart will only attain to perfection in entering into these designs of Providence and cooperating in this general movement. May not the active members take courage from the thought, that while they are visiting the sick, and fighting manfully against Satan for the souls of the dying, a Community is there, like Moses on the hill, lifting up its hands to draw down blessings from Heaven on their warfare. O Sacred Heart of Jesus, arm them for the contest, fill their hearts with dauntless perseverance, let prayer be ever on their lips, and strength in their arms, deliver them from that carelessness and apathy which grieve the Holy Spirit, let them not be overcome by sloth during the agony of Thy members, as Thy Disciples were overcome by sleep in Thine own Agony!

CHAPTER VI.

THE WORK IN COMMUNITIES.

This work flourishes best in Communities, because their members are most like Jesus in His Agony. The resemblance strengthened by devotion to His Agonising Heart. Zeal of active Communities for our object; and of contemplative Communities.

JUST as a plant has a special soil and climate in which its blossoms and its fruits attain the greatest perfection, so each Devotion has a chosen home, where God makes it prosper more particularly. Devotion to the Agonising Heart of Jesus attains a greater development in the cloister, especially in the souls of its most fervent inmates; and its fruits are gathered by the dying.

Why is that its chosen home? Because interior sufferings, martyrdom of the heart, spiritual agonies, are to be found among the members of Religious Communities more than among the laity. Is it not meet that those who aim at perfection should be made like the Divine Model of perfection, and consequently that they should follow Him in the Agonies which He suffered from His Incarnation to His Death? Those who have no domestic ties escape many of the external trials to which Christians living in their families are exposed. A Christian in the world is exposed to suffering on all sides. It may come through his children, or the companion of his life; through his honour, his interests, or his care for the future of those dear to him. A Religious has forsaken all things, suffering has less hold on him, the very regularity of his life preserves him from many maladies. Nevertheless, a vow is on him to bear the Cross daily; he pursues it. When he entered on the path of the evangelical counsels, he made choice of the Cross that he might gain Jesus. Can he then fail to find it? It will come to him surely, not, it may be, from without, but it will penetrate within and take possession of his heart. Jesus will indeed give Himself to him, but at the same time He will give him a share in His Agony. A Religious in his cell has this resemblance to our Lord in the Grotto on the Mount of Olives, that he suffers a secret martyrdom, and while he suffers he prays to God, and he loves all mankind. Must not his heart be brought into contact with the Agonising Heart of Jesus, that its resemblance to that Divine Model may be perfected?

Devotion to the Agonising Heart does this. As it takes root in the heart of the disciple, it produces in it conformity to the Heart of the Master, it makes him ready to encounter interior struggles, and helps him to sanctify himself by those trials which prove the ruin of so many souls. We believe it to have a special providential mission amongst Religious Orders in this age of egotism. It tends to preserve in them a spirit of self-renunciation and sacrifice, by bringing them continually back to the very source of abnegation—the Heart of Jesus. This, no doubt, is the reason of the zeal with which the children of St. Ignatius, and the double family of St. Vincent de Paul, have adopted and propagated this Devotion and that of the Holy Agony, which honours the same mystery. We give a few facts regarding the first. Of all active Congregations the first to embrace it with great ardour was that of Sainte-Chrétienne, which has several Houses in the north of France. Sister Sainte-Amable, whom God has since taken to Himself, had a burning zeal for the honour of the Divine Heart. She did much to spread this Devotion in the north, particularly amongst her Sisters in Religion. Another Nun, named Saint-Régis, of the House of Sédan, gave the invocation and veneration of the Agonising Heart a definite form among work-women and others. Much good was thus done amongst the Religious themselves, their pupils, and people in the world; in fact, amongst all who were brought into relation with this House. The same happy fruits have been gathered by other active Communities; for example, among the pupils in the Convent of our Lady, at Saint Leónard, Haute Vienne; in the Hospital of Saint Alexis at Limoges, and in the Orphanage of Nazareth attached to the same Community. It is touching to see the fidelity and ardour of the little orphans in taking their turn of intercession for the agonising of each day.

Contemplative Communities can also bear witness to the benefits of this Devotion. Mere speculative, philosophic contemplation would not of itself lead to that supernatural union with God which gives us so mighty a power over His Heart, both for our own sanctification and for the conversion of sinners. Thinking often of God in this manner is a means to union, but only a means. The devils and lost souls think of God more than we do, and yet they can never attain to union with Him. The contemplative life, in the full Christian sense of the term, implies above all things a loving contemplation, for love is at once its principle and its end. Now, love of God necessarily tends to union with God; and the contemplative life, by all its exercises, develops this tendency. A soul which follows them faithfully, unites itself more and more closely to God, loves God more and more, and gains more and more power over

His Heart. And are not the different practices of the Devotion to the Agonising Heart of Jesus so many exercises of union; union in love, and union in suffering, union even in those things most contrary to our nature, in grievous sadness, in weariness, in desolation, in fear and trouble, in keen and protracted sufferings? Therefore it is welcomed in cloisters with an eagerness which the Heart of our Master fails not to reward. Let us mention, as examples, La Trappe of Montélimar, where a person who generously assisted the infant Community of the Agonising Heart has taken the vows, under the name of Sister Ephrene; the Carmel of Rennes, which printed the statutes of our Association; the Monastery of the Visitation at Vienna; the Nuns of the Visitation at Mans, who are members of the Confraternity established in their church, who keep the register of Associates, and offer special prayers each day for the dying who are recommended to them. Many other Religious Houses might be mentioned where chapels have been dedicated to the Agonising Heart of Jesus.

It is much to be wished that this Devotion were firmly established in every Community, so that the Religious themselves, and those with whom they have to do, might fully enter into it. Might they not, with the permission of their Bishops, form Associations in their churches, and have them affiliated to the Archconfraternity at Jerusalem? Or, if this plan should present too many difficulties, might they not send their names to some Confraternity already existing?

CHAPTER VII.

GRACES OBTAINED.

Blessings connected with the worship of the Sacred Heart. Blessings received by the Associates of the Agonising Heart. Their special happiness in Heaven. Graces which they gain for others. Examples.

THE Devotion of the Agonising Heart of Jesus shares in those benedictions promised by our Lord to the general Devotion to the Sacred Heart, of which it is a branch. Our Lord said to the Blessed Margaret Mary: "I promise you that My Heart will open to shed abundant influence of divine love on those who pay It this honour, and lead others to do so."* This holy Virgin was so persuaded of the reality of the revelation that she went on to say—"Such grace will be gained by Religious Orders from this Devotion, that no other means will be required for the restoration of fervour and regularity in the most relaxed Communities, or for the complete perfection of those who are strictly faithful to their vows. My Divine Saviour showed me that those who labour for the

* Languet, *La Vie de la B. Marguerite Marie*, l. iv.

salvation of souls will have the art of touching the most hardened hearts, and will obtain marvellous success, if they are themselves filled with devotion to His Divine Heart. Those who live in the world will obtain the graces needful for their state, that is to say, peace in their families, support in their toils, and the blessing of God on all their undertakings. The adorable Heart will be their place of refuge during life, and especially at the hour of their death."* The Agonising Heart of Jesus is indeed a refuge and a source of abundant graces to the Associates. It gives them patience and strength in their trials, consolation and joy in their sorrows, a burning and generous love for the Saviour Who, having suffered in His own Person, still suffers in that of His members. Their intentions become more pure, their zeal more active, their fear of death more salutary, their desire to console the Divine Sufferer more ardent, their joy in winning souls greater and more heartfelt. But grace is essentially invisible, and very often the Associates are not aware in this world of all the supernatural assistance they have received; in Heaven they will see what this Devotion has gained for them. There they will enjoy happiness of a special kind, not the less real in its nature because it forms only a part of their accidental beatitude. The Founder of the work speaks of it as follows:—"To form

* Languet, *Vie de la B. Marguerite Marie*, l. vi.

an idea of this happiness, and to quicken our desires for it, we must remember that among the Elect in Heaven there are not only different degrees but also different kinds of bliss. Is there not in the world a great difference between the joys of a child and of a father, between those of a subject and of a sovereign? Besides the father's individual happiness, has he not a special pleasure in seeing himself surrounded by a loving and beloved family? There is something of the same kind in Heaven. There are parental joys for those who have been the means of bringing others to eternal life. Those who have laboured exclusively for their own salvation will be happy, no doubt, but those who have laboured at the same time for the salvation of others will have a joy beyond that which is common to all the Saints. For, as God the Father gives earthly fathers a certain share in the prerogatives and joys of His Paternity, so the Son of God, the Saviour, associates with Himself some chosen souls, who with Him and by Him *save* the world. As King and Father of all the Elect He rejoices in the joy of all His children, and He is glorious in their glory. After Jesus, Mary the Queen and Mother of the Elect is happy in their bliss and glorious in their glory. Then come the Apostles, that is to say, all those who openly or secretly have participated in the Saviour's work of restoration. And amongst

K

their number I see souls unknown to the world, whose fervent prayers and whose union with Jesus Christ have helped to people Heaven. The bliss of these souls is beyond what we can conceive. It is multiplied by the number they have saved. If your prayers have gained salvation for twenty or thirty of the dying, your happiness in Heaven will be twenty or thirty times more perfect than if you had not prayed for them."*

But the graces on which we would dwell above all are those gained for the sick and dying. God only can tell their number, for He only knows to what prayers and efforts He has been pleased to grant the conversion of any dying person. Sometimes, at the last moment, a mystery of love takes place between the guilty soul and its Judge; this may be a fruit of our intercessions. An author who had gained a sad kind of celebrity, and had been the declared enemy of a great Religious Order and a promoter of the Italian Revolution, was struck by sudden death. We have often been told that after his death he appeared to one of these Religious, who lived a very holy life at Naples, and said to him—"I am not lost; I have had time to make an act of contrition, and I owe this grace to the prayers which you all make for your enemies." The devoted friends

* *Devotion au Cœur Agonisant de Jésus*, ch. vi. Avignon, 1850, in 18.

of the Saviour's Agonising Heart may thus obtain by their supplications many hidden graces and unknown conversions. The living are witnesses of many most precious though not always extraordinary favours gained by them for the dying.

At Limoges, in the beginning of the year 1862, the Nuns of St. Alexis wrote : "Since we have embraced the Devotion to the Agonising Heart of Jesus and the compassionate Heart of Mary, we have found it to be a source of most precious and abundant graces for ourselves and also for the poor sick in our great hospital. We no longer have the grief of seeing the dying refuse the last sacraments. When we have to deal with the most hardened sinners we pray to the Sacred Hearts of Jesus and Mary for them, and are immediately answered."*

A letter from the Superior of the Visitation of Sainte Marie, at Mans, dated March 4, 1864, gives the following testimony : "As to the fruit produced by this pious Confraternity, we can affirm that it is immense. We do not enumerate details, but we know that holy deaths are often due to it. We have experienced this in the case of our dear Sisters, whom we have had the consolation to see at their last moments in the most satisfactory state of mind."

Another letter, written by the Superior of the

* *Messager du Sacré Cœur*, art. iv., p. 81. Juillet, 1862.

Agonising Heart, at Mende, on the 6th of March in the same year, says : "We know that many conversions have been obtained, but the details have not always a special interest. One thing is certain, that since the establishment of the Association in this place, and more particularly since the foundation of our House, an improvement has been observed in the minds of the dying, and, except in cases of sudden death, no one has died without the sacraments. A man under sentence of death, whose state of mind was most deplorable, has at last yielded to grace, and has consoled us by his penitence as much as he had previously appalled us by his impiety."

We proceed to relate some cases of special interest. They will serve to show what graces may be expected from the Agonising Heart of our good Master.

CHAPTER VIII.

THE DYING CONVERTED.

Conversion of two old men, one rich and the other poor, one at home and the other in a hospital.

TOWARDS the end of the year 1857, in the town of ——, a devoted member of our Confraternity was attending the death-bed of a man sixty-one years of age. He was a very learned man, but ignorant of the ways of salvation. He used to say—" If any one presumes to bring a Priest to see me I shall manage to get rid of him at once; I have enough strength left to throw him out of the window. My principles are well known; I intend to die as I have lived!" Some one having tried to speak to him of a Priest, his answer was—" If you mention those people to me again, I forbid you my house."

His friend recommended him to the prayers of the Association. This was done at seven o'clock in the evening. The night passed quietly. In the morning the sick man asked to see the doctor, who found him in the greatest danger. He then sent for the person who had spoken to him formerly about religion, and said: "I am not of the same mind that I was yesterday. You have spoken to me of the mercy of God, you have told me that He is always ready to receive the greatest sinners. If this be true, go for a Priest, and make haste or it will be too late." He was told that many prayers had been offered for him, and expressed gratitude for them.

A venerable Priest came with all speed, and soon after he went to bring the Blessed Sacrament. In the meantime the dying man desired that all the flowers in his garden should be gathered, to adorn his room and the places through which the Blessed Sacrament would pass. We cannot describe his transports of joy and gratitude on seeing It arrive. Many of those who followed burst into tears, and their emotion was increased when they heard this happy penitent express his great grief for having offended God, beg pardon from those around him for the offence he had given them, and request them to tell their acquaintance of his real repentance. Afterwards he told his Confessor that he regretted but one thing, namely, not to have even a year to make amends for his former evil life.

When he was about to receive the Holy Communion, he repeated three times in French the *Domine non sum dignus*, with a mingled expression of sorrow and joy. "Is it possible," said he, "that God will condescend to come into a heart so defiled as mine?" After the Communion he asked for Extreme Unction. His Confessor administered it with joy, and says that he can never forget the consolation this conversion gave him. Nothing more remained to be done, and in a quarter of an hour he went to Heaven to sing the mercies of the Lord for ever.*

In the month of March, 1861, a man of sixty years of age went to the Hospital of St. Alexis, at Limoges. He was suffering from an acute malady, and he was a hardened sinner. We give the story of his conversion as we have had it from the Nuns:—

"The old man was placed in St. Vincent's

* *Le Cœur Agonisant de Jésus*, 5e edit., p. 46—50.

ward. The Sister in charge was preparing the sick for their Easter duties; she spoke to the new comer of receiving the sacraments, but from his answer she perceived at once that he was without religion. She asked for prayers for him, and we trusted in the Agonising Heart of Jesus and the compassionate Heart of Mary that the moment of grace would come. But great was our grief when, during the beautiful Month of Mary, his state became most alarming, and he repulsed us with even unusual obstinacy. He refused to kiss the crucifix, and the hard and cutting words with which he met any effort made in his behalf cost the good Sister many tears.

"The Chaplains had done everything that zeal could do. The doctors and medical students had also tried to gain him; even the other sick men in the ward, shocked at the prospect of his unhappy death, had represented to him how wrong he was in refusing the good advice of the devoted Sisters. 'You see,' added these poor people, 'what the Sister says is true. She proves it by coming to serve us, for she would not do so unless the good God, to Whom she wishes to bring you back, had not put it into her heart.' 'Leave me alone,' was his constant answer; 'Priests and Nuns are a bad set.'

"Things were in this state, and the sick man got worse and worse. We were more and more afraid, thinking that this poor man might die at any moment. We made ceaseless intercessions to the Agonising Heart of Jesus. We turned also to the compassionate Heart of our divine Mother, the Refuge of Sinners and the Channel of Grace. We prayed with great confidence, and said—'O Lord, can it be that Thou hast intrusted this man to our care, and let him come by a particular permission of Thy providence, to this holy house, and yet that he is not to share the favours abundantly showered down here? Oh no, my God, Thou canst not refuse our prayers; this poor sinner will not surely die a reprobate.'

"The beautiful Feast of the Ascension drew near. The same impenitency continued; the dying man grew worse, and we doubted if he could live through the day. We had no resource but redoubled prayers. For a long time the intercession which we make every day from half-past two to three o'clock had been specially offered for the conversion of this soul; that day we chose a Sister who was fervent and devoted to the Agonising Heart above all others. It was the time for Vespers, and we left her in our little oratory to pour forth her supplication.

"After Vespers, our Chaplain, M. Martin, went into the pulpit. He was to preach on the Feast of the day, but instead of beginning his subject, he said, in a voice half choked with tears—'My brethren, during the eighteen years of my ministry I have never seen anything like the hardness and impenitence shown at this moment by a sick man who is at the point of death. We have prayed, we have wept, we have exhorted him, but all has been in vain. Let us pray again, my brethren, for this soul has cost the blood of the Son of God. "Most holy Virgin, present our humble supplications to the Divine Majesty and we shall be heard. You can refuse us nothing in this beautiful month, which is dedicated to you."' M. Henry, our Superior and Vicar-General, rose and asked all present to say a *Pater* and an *Ave.* (People attend the Offices in the beautiful church of this hospital, which is consecrated to the Agonising Heart of Jesus.) All present fell on their knees and prayed fervently, many shed tears.

"At this moment the hardened sinner's heart was miraculously changed. The Sister in charge of the ward went straight to him when she left the church. 'My good man,' said she, 'you are suffering a great deal; say what I tell you and you will be relieved: "My God, have mercy on me."' And for the first time, without making any objection, he repeated the words after her. Encouraged by this change, she proceeded: '"My God, I am very sorry for having offended Thee; I believe in Thee, I hope in Thee, I love Thee with all my heart. Holy Virgin, my good Mother, have pity on me. Good St. Joseph, pray for me."' He repeated it all. The

Sister was delighted, and said in her heart—
'O Agonising Heart of Jesus, Thy merits have saved this soul from hell.' The very countenance of the sick man had a different expression. M. Martin came in, and the poor man begged him to hear his confession. The good Priest encouraged and consoled him, embraced him, heard his confession, and gave him Extreme Unction and the Holy Viaticum. He was with him till he breathed his last on the following day.

"This dying man was sincerely converted. He seemed happy whenever the Sister came near him. He joined in her prayers, he kissed the crucifix, which he had before refused to look at, and spoke of his happiness to those around him."*

CHAPTER IX.

OTHER EXAMPLES.

Conversion of a young man who had resisted grace. Conversion of an impious blasphemer. Reflections of a Religious.

WE give two other conversions related by the same Nuns :—

"About the end of October, 1861, we received into the hospital a young man in

* *Messager du Sacré Cœur*, Juillet, 1862, art. iv., p. 81—84.

consumption; he was placed in St. Peter's Ward. A month later his state became alarming. He refused to go to confession. The disease made rapid progress, and the Sister was very uneasy about him. He was well instructed, as he had been studying for the Priesthood, and she saw that it was resistance to grace which had brought his soul into so deplorable a state.

"We applied, as we always do, to the Agonising Heart of Jesus and the compassionate Heart of Mary. Our half-hour of intercession, our Communions, our prayers, were offered for him; we constantly repeated the invocations, 'O most merciful Jesus,' &c., and 'O most merciful Mary,' &c. Remembering the many graces They had already granted, we continued to hope.

"But one day the Sister found him so ill that she felt it her duty to speak more strongly than she had yet done. 'You weary me, my Sister, the Chaplain has also wearied me; let me be quiet,' this was his only answer. Soon afterwards a fit of weakness came on, he was thought to be near death, and seemed rather alarmed. The nurse of the infirmary had been charged by the Sister to call her if a favourable change seemed likely to take place, and while she attended him, she spoke to him of God, and prayed for him.

"On the following day, when our good Mother paid her visit to the hospital, she met the doctor and the Sister in charge of the dispensary. The Sister seemed so agitated, that the Superior asked her what was the matter. 'That poor man,' she said, 'will die to-day, and he refuses the last sacraments.' The doctor said, 'It is true that he cannot live through the day.' Our Mother hastened to him to make a last effort, but great was her surprise and joy when after listening to a few kind words, he begged for a Priest to hear his confession.

"The Priest was soon there, and the sick man, touched by an irresistible impulse of grace, received the sacraments in the best possible state of mind. Contrary to all expectations, God prolonged his life for a few days, no doubt to give him the opportunity of repairing the offence which he had given to his companions in the ward.

"Is not this conversion a miracle of grace, due to the infinite merits of our Divine Saviour, Who suffered so bitter an Agony for the salvation of sinners? We cannot doubt that supplications to the Agonising Heart of Jesus and the compassionate Heart of Mary are always heard. Blessed and praised eternally be those Sacred Hearts, to whose service we consecrate ourselves for ever. Amen."*

About the middle of the year 1863, the good Nuns recounted another conversion :—

* *Messager du Sacré Cœur*, Juillet, 1862, art. iv., p. 85—87.

"We had in the hospital a sick man named Peillaraud (*patois* for rag-man). His body was covered with dreadful ulcers, and the state of his soul was far more deplorable.

"For many years he had obstinately resisted every endeavour to bring him back to the right path. He could not bear to hear God spoken of, he laughed at religion, he tried to prevent others, and answered by blasphemies any attempt made to console him. When the Sister in charge of the ward had finished the catechism which is daily repeated there, he used to begin a parody on it, evidently inspired by the Evil One himself. We prayed and waited long, and at last we trusted that a Mission which was to be given at the hospital in the month of March, would change this heart of stone. All in vain; the example of the other sick people, and the zeal of the Missionaries, were of no effect. He would not even speak civilly to the good Fathers, and they were obliged in sorrow to give him up. No one in the house ventured any more to mention the sacraments, or, indeed, the subject of religion at all to him.

"Nevertheless, we continued to place our confidence in the Agonising Heart of Jesus, through the compassionate Heart of Mary. We were not dismayed. Our Divine Master and His tender Mother were moved by our constant prayers. Nothing but a miracle could reach this case, and it was granted.

"A sudden and irresistible grace impelled this poor sinner to send for one of our good Priests, whom he had so often insulted. He said he wanted to make his confession at once. The first day it took two hours. Before long he had the happiness of receiving the Holy Viaticum and Extreme Unction, and the Bishop kindly came to the ward to confirm him. He made reparation for the offence he had given, and his death was full of consolation to us. Love, honour, praise, and glory be to the Agonising Heart of our Divine Master, and to the compassionate Heart of the Mother of Mercies."*

We cannot do better than conclude by giving our readers the reflections of a Religious on these and similar instances of conversion :—

"It was indeed a heavenly inspiration which led Father Lyonnard to establish the Devotion to the Agonising Heart of Jesus. The dying are too much neglected by Christians. This is a great misfortune, and one which we must endeavour to remedy by prayer and devotedness. The devil always, like a lion seizing his prey, redoubles his efforts at the awful moment which decides the soul's eternal fate. You know what infernal means he takes to prevent a Priest approaching to the dying, what a system of machinations he employs to keep souls at a

* *Messager du Sacré Cœur*, Juillet, 1863, art. vii., p. 47, 48.

distance from God till death overtakes them. Everywhere, alas! we see relations and friends deterred by sinful fear from speaking of God to the sick who are about to appear before Him. They shrink from giving a painful shock; and so they leave the soul in ignorance of its real state, sliding into the bottomless pit, unwarned, unaided; they will wait till the death-rattle is heard, and till consciousness is gone, before they call for a Priest, who can then only give absolution and Extreme Unction with the sad probability of those sacraments being unavailing.

"But it is a sad mistake to think that speaking of God saddens people. The soul is, as Tertullian says, naturally Christian; and if there is a time when its immortal aspirations are stronger than another, it is at the moment of contact with eternity. No one knows what heavenly attractions, what appeals of grace, are felt by a soul on the point of returning to its Creator and Saviour. No one knows the penitence, the holy recollections, the hopes that may be awakened in that hour when the enemies of salvation are making a last effort to frustrate God's redeeming work; but when He Who shed His Blood for the soul is supporting it with even unusual aid, perhaps one word of warning and advice given to that soul at such a moment might be the means of its conversion, and of its eternal welfare.

"Oh! would that we knew the full value of

a soul, the necessity of the means established in the Church for the restoration of lost grace, the greatness of that divine holiness with which we must be clothed to appear before God, we should then hesitate no longer; we should exhort urgently, and at any cost, and we should gain the victory, a victory of eternal salvation for the souls that we love."*

CHAPTER X.

ARCHCONFRATERNITY AT JERUSALEM.

All hearts are turned towards Jerusalem. A young person invokes the Agonising Heart for her dying father; causes a medal to be struck; wishes for the establishment of an Archconfraternity at Jerusalem; corresponds with Father Lyonnard. The Patriarch, Mgr. Valerga, views the project with favour. Its execution delayed by difficulties.

THE Prophet Isaiah declared of old, that the sepulchre of Christ should be glorious (Isa. xi. 10), and in fulfilment of this prediction, Christians, during many centuries, might be seen gathering in the guise of humble pilgrims around the tomb of their Redeemer, and visiting the other spots which His presence had consecrated; and when these holy places had fallen under the dominion of the Mahometans, they

* *Messager du Sacré Cœur*, Février, 1864., art. v., p. 88—90.

went forth valiantly to do battle for their deliverance.

At the present day all Christian hearts are drawn towards Jerusalem. Heretics and schismatics, Germans, English, and Russians, vie with Catholics in pressing towards the Holy City, in getting possession of a corner of ground, and establishing a chapel or sanctuary there. The very tumult and discord heard around the Holy Sepulchre, are a homage paid by all nations, tongues, sects, and rites, to the tomb of One Who was more than a sage, more than a hero, more than a man—to the Incarnate Son of God, who died for the world's salvation.

The increased facility of communication in our days has revived the custom of pilgrimages to Palestine, but at all periods the thoughts and affections of the Faithful have centred in Jerusalem. Just as churches were formerly turned to the east, in order that the Priest, when offering to God the Adorable Victim, might look towards the guest-chamber where the Lord's Supper was first celebrated, and towards Calvary, where that same Victim first offered Himself, so all true Christian hearts turn to the east, to Sion, to the Mount of Olives, to Golgotha, when they offer their daily Sacrifices to God in union with the Sacrifice made by our Blessed Saviour. The idea of establishing the Association of the Agonising Heart of Jesus as an Archconfraternity arose in the mind of a pious person whose sorrows had made her mind dwell on the thought of Jerusalem.

She saw her beloved father almost at the point of death, without having attempted to make his peace with God. Her filial piety, her ardent faith, her natural affection, all combined to overwhelm her with unspeakable sorrow. The thought of the Agony of Jesus made her implore that merciful Saviour Who had undergone so much physical and moral Agony for our sakes, to save the soul of her father, and to relieve her cruel anxiety on his account. This double grace was granted her, and in her transport of gratitude and joy she longed to persuade all the afflicted, especially those whose friends are taken from them, to have recourse to the same Divine Comforter. She wished to glorify the Agonising Heart of Jesus to induce the Faithful to show new marks of confidence and of love.

She thought of having a medal struck in memory of our Lord's Agony in the Garden of Olives. A pious friend, already well known by her devotion to Jesus in the Sacrament of His Love, defrayed the first expenses, and had the medal struck by Alcan, and when she went to Rome presented it to Pius IX., who had already approved of the design. The Holy Father, on receiving it, said, " Here is the medal that suits me!" He granted by word of mouth to this medal all the indulgences granted to others by himself and his predecessors. It has been widely spread, and has helped to promote the Devotion to the Agonising Heart.

The idea of the Archconfraternity at Jerusalem had, as we have said, occurred to the pious lady who originated the medal. It seemed to her that the afflicted might be led to turn their eyes to the Garden of Gethsemane, and to draw strength for their different necessities from the Agonising Heart of the Divine Saviour. But the Founder of our Devotion had forestalled her. From the first he had seen the advantage of making the Association an Archconfraternity. He had written several times on the subject to the Father General of the Society of Jesus, at Rome. The Nuns of the Visitation at Mans had also petitioned that the Association already established in their church might be elevated into an Archconfraternity. The power and the gentleness of the workings of Providence may be traced throughout. The fervent Religious and the pious lady, who were attracted to the Garden of Olives by similar motives, were now brought into communication with each other. Her desire was that all the afflicted might find consolation in the Agonies of the Divine Heart. while he sought especially the crowning consolation, the grace of a holy death for all the dying. They were united in the purpose of honouring the Agonising Heart of their Lord by a special worship of compassion and of love.

Father Lyonnard and this devout soul agreed

together as to the nature of the new Archconfraternity. The Father drew up a formulary, mentioning the privileges and indulgences which they wished to obtain from the Sovereign Pontiff. It was submitted to Mgr. Foulquier, Bishop of Mende; our Lord was pleased to give this holy and devoted Prelate the consolation of forwarding an enterprise so well fitted to promote His glory and the salvation of souls. He encouraged the authors of this pious project, approved of the formulary, and sent it to the Patriarch of Jerusalem, earnestly begging His Eminence to take the matter into consideration, and to use his influence in recommending it to the Sovereign Pontiff. Mgr. Valerga replied with much goodwill, and promised to do all in his power for the establishment of the Archconfraternity at Jerusalem.

On the 11th of October, 1863, M. l'Abbé Dequevauviller, his Vicar-General, wrote as follows:—" His Eminence is most anxious that the Archconfraternity of the Agonising Heart of Jesus should be attached to the church whose foundations were laid two years ago, but which is still unfinished for want of funds. The walls of the choir and the two side chapels are finished as far as the vaulting. One of the side chapels is destined for the future Archconfraternity, and when it is completed Monseigneur will endeavour to obtain from the Holy See the spiritual favours desired."

The Patriarch himself wrote on the 4th of December in the same year:—"I wish to encourage the establishment of this pious Archconfraternity at Jerusalem; but there are difficulties in the way which cannot at once be overcome. Remember that there are only about twelve hundred Catholics in Jerusalem, and that several Associations or Confraternities already exist. In order to forward the present project, I think it will be well to amalgamate the existing Congregation of our Lady of Seven Dolours with the Archconfraternity of the Agonising Heart of Jesus. This change must be gradual, and one necessary condition which we hope to see fulfilled in the course of the year 1864 is the completion of the three principal chapels of our new church. Some of the religious ceremonies of the Confraternity might be performed in the Holy Grotto in the Garden of Olives, which is about half an hour's distance outside the walls of the town, and I willingly consent to have the principal chapel of the Patriarchal church consecrated to this touching mystery of the Passion. But before the Archconfraternity of the Agonising Heart of Jesus can be erected at Jerusalem, we must first have a simple Confraternity, to which, by Apostolic concession, the Confraternities already existing, or hereafter to be founded in France, may be associated."

CHAPTER XI.

ARCHCONFRATERNITY AT JERUSALEM.

Decree of the Patriarch establishing the Confraternity. Indulgences granted by the Pope. How to become a member. First consequence, propagation of Devotion to the Agonising Heart. Second consequence, the diffusion of the general Devotion to the Sacred Heart. Egotism and self-indulgence will be thus diminished by this Devotion.

THE simple Confraternity spoken of in the preceding letter was established by a Rescript, of which we give the translation :—

Joseph Valerga, by divine mercy, and the favour of the Apostolic See, Patriarch of Jerusalem, Vicar-Apostolic, Delegate of the Holy See, &c. &c.

Amidst the various afflictions which trouble the present age, every Christian soul may find many most powerful motives of consolation in devout and constant meditation on the Sorrows and the Passion of our Redeemer Jesus Christ. Moved by this consideration, some pious souls desire to form a holy society, with the object of paying a special worship to the most afflicted Heart of Jesus, so overwhelmed with sorrows throughout His whole life, and enduring so fearful an Agony in the Garden of Olives, in order to gain, by their prayers, in virtue of the infinite merits of that holy Agony, the grace of a happy death for all the dying throughout the world; and lastly, to draw, from the contemplation of the most loving Heart of our Saviour, Which is the source of all consolation, strength and courage to meet the troubles of life. They would have every one learn from It the power of divine resignation under all circumstances; they would have all turn to It for real, holy, and lasting consolation in suffering.

THE CONFRATERNITY.

The value of such a Confraternity must be great at any time, but it is especially manifest in the present days of trouble and perturbation, when society is passing through sad vicissitudes, and many persons remain until death indifferent to their salvation. Desirous that the Faithful committed to our charge should have a share in all the graces and spiritual benefits which this Confraternity procures, or may hereafter procure, and yielding willingly to the ardent request of a large number of Christians, we receive this Confraternity into our Patriarchal diocese, we approve of it, and, in virtue of our authority, by these endowments we establish it in this holy city of Jerusalem.

But seeing that the number of the Faithful in this city is too small to allow of the multiplication of Confraternities, the members of the old Confraternity of the Blessed Virgin Mary have promptly and willingly entered the new Confraternity. As the practices of the one in no way interfere with, but rather forward, the objects of the other, we cannot but approve of this manifestation of their zeal. Therefore, in virtue of the present Rescript, we unite these two Confraternities under the title of the Most Sacred Heart of our Lord Jesus Christ Agonising in the Garden of Olives, and of the Transfixion of the Blessed Virgin Mary, with the statutes which we shall sanction. We exhort all the Faithful under our care to embrace this Devotion heartily for the good of their souls.

Given at Jerusalem, in our Patriarchal palace, the 14th of June, 1864.

Some time afterwards the Abbé Dequevauviller wrote as follows to the Superior of the Agonising Heart at Mende :—"I am happy to inform you that our dear Confraternity of the Agonising Heart of Jesus was established at Jerusalem two months ago, and I am glad to add that it is working admirably. The Associates meet every Sunday in the new chapel of the Agonising Heart of Jesus, and we daily expect from Rome a picture of this touching mystery."

On the 14th of August in the same year, in an audience given to the secretary of the Sacred Congregation of the Propaganda, His Holiness Pope Pius IX. was pleased to grant a plenary indulgence, applicable to the souls in Purgatory, on the following days, to all the Faithful of both sexes who are members of the Confraternity at Jerusalem, canonically established under the title of the Most Sacred Agonising Heart of Jesus, and of the Transfixion of the Blessed Virgin Mary, provided that in a devout frame of mind they confess their sins, receive Holy Communion, visit some church, chapel, or public oratory on the said days, praying there a certain length of time for the propagation of our holy faith:—

On the day of admission, the Feast of the Prayer of our Lord on the Mount of Olives, the two Feasts of the Precious Blood of Jesus Christ, the Feast of the Five Wounds and of the Most Holy Sacrament, Holy Thursday, the Feast of the Sacred Heart, the two Feasts of the Transfixion of Mary—that is to say, of our Lady of Seven Dolours, the Feast of St. Joseph, and of his Patronage, and also at the hour of death, provided that in a proper state of mind they devoutly invoke the Holy Name of Jesus

THE CONFRATERNITY. 133

with their lips, or, if they cannot speak, at least in their hearts.

In the following year, one of the Fathers of the Society of Jesus, who has a special zeal for the honour of the Agonising Heart and for the salvation of the dying, distributed a printed paper, urgently inviting Christians to join this Confraternity at Jerusalem. In an autograph letter to the Rev. Father Boué, His Excellency the Patriarch had expressed his desire to see many of the Bishops establish the Confraternity in their dioceses, and ask for the indulgences granted to that of the Holy City.

At length the long-desired Archconfraternity was established, by a Brief dated August, 1867, of which we subjoin a translation :—

PIUS IX., POPE.
FOR A PERPETUAL REMEMBRANCE.

The Roman Pontiffs have never ceased to favour, by proofs of their paternal affection, and to enrich with special honours, privileges, and indulgences, the Lay Confraternities, established in the name of the Lord for the performance of holy and pious works, which are of so great ornament and service to the Church of God. Hence, having been informed by our beloved son, the Cardinal Prefect of the Congregation of the Propaganda, that, by the praiseworthy zeal of our Venerable Brother, Joseph, Patriarch of Jerusalem, a pious Confraternity of the Agonising Heart of Jesus and the Dolours of the Blessed Virgin Mary has been established at Jerusalem some years ago, to obtain for those who are in their last agony the grace of a happy death, and having been entreated to enrich the afore-mentioned Confraternity with the title and privileges of an Archconfraternity, in order that so salutary an institute may, by God's blessing, be more widely extended, We, wishing to testify our singular goodwill to all and every one whom these letters concern, and absolving them, and considering them absolved, by the mere effect of this present letter, from all sentences of excommunication, interdict, or other ecclesiastical censures and penalties, in whatever way or for whatever cause passed against them, should they have incurred any, by our Apostolic authority in virtue of these present letters, establish and constitute in perpetuity the Confraternity established at Jerusalem, under the title of the Agonising Heart of Jesus and the Dolours of the Blessed Virgin Mary, as an Archconfraternity, with all the accustomed rights, privileges, honours, pre-eminences, and indulgences. We grant also to the Directors, or the Officers and Associates, present and future, of the same Confraternity, thus established into an Archconfraternity, the power of aggregating to the said Archconfraternity, with the express consent of the Patriarch of Jerusalem for the time being, other Confraternities of the same name and institute, wherever they may be, except within our city of Rome, with the permission of the Ordinary, observing the Constitution *Quæcumque* of Clement VIII., our predecessor, and the Decree of the Congregation of Indulgences, issued on the 8th of January, 1861 ; and we give to them the power of communicating to them all the indulgences granted by the Apostolic See to the aforesaid Confraternity, and others which are communicable, freely, lawfully, and in perpetuity.

Notwithstanding all things to the contrary, even those deserving special and individual modification.

Given at Rome, at St. Peter's, under the ring of the Fisherman, August the 23rd, 1867, the twenty-second year of our Pontificate.

N. CARD. PARACCIANI CLARELLI.

(Locus Sigilli).

The Faithful who wish to enter the Archconfraternity of Jerusalem, but who find a difficulty in sending their names directly there, may send them to the Director of the Eastern schools, at Paris, or to the Superior of the Agonising Heart, at Lyons, either of whom will faithfully forward them.*

The more the Archconfraternity spreads throughout the whole Church, the greater results may be expected to follow.

We will say a few words regarding these results. The first will be the wide and rapid propagation of devotion to the Agonising Heart of Jesus. Grace makes use of natural means for the extension of its empire. A devotion or practice of piety which is recommended by a great name, or associated with a celebrated place, shines with a kind of reflected light, and finds a readier access into people's minds. The memory of a Saint keeps alive the works which he has founded, and there are certain towns whose influence is felt far and wide. Rome and Jerusalem have this glorious privilege, as well as many other common characteristics. Both are, as it were, separated from the world by a desert, both are full of ruins which show that they have been more than once the prey

* A M. le Directeur des Ecoles d'Orient, 12, Rue du Regard, Paris. A Mdme. la Supérieure du Cœur-Agonisant, Quartier de Monplaisir, aux Quatre-Maisons, 11, Lyon.

of conquerors, and both have preserved intact some remains of former days. Who can fail to have his heart touched when he visits the catacombs at Rome, in which the early Christians used to assemble; the amphitheatre where the Martyrs died; and the prison where St. Peter was a captive? Or again, who is not moved to tears when amidst the many holy places of Jerusalem, which have been transformed and beautified, he sees those which still remain in their primitive condition, such as the grotto where St. Peter wept over his fault, and the Garden of Gethsemane, where Jesus watered with His drops of Blood some of those very olive trees which are still standing? We welcome all that Rome sends us, and Christians will also hail an Archconfraternity coming from Jerusalem, from the very scene of the mystery offered to their veneration, and from the very spot where the Divine Saviour Himself died.

The second consequence will be the wider spread of the general Devotion to the Sacred Heart through all grades of Christian society. Our Lord revealed this Devotion for the benefit of all; He wished that all should share His love and His graces, so that their love to Him might never grow cold. Have His intentions been completely fulfilled? It would seem not, for this admirable Devotion is as yet confined to a chosen number of pious souls. Constant and praiseworthy efforts are made, not only to enlarge its sphere, but also to make it penetrate more deeply; that is to say, to propagate it in countries where it is little known, and among those lukewarm Christians who think they are doing great things if they only observe the precepts of the decalogue. It will revive the fire of divine love in their hearts; it will awaken their generosity. Will not such cold hearts open the more readily to receive a Devotion which comes before them in its most striking, most tangible, and most sympathetic form? The constant appeal to our sorrowful Saviour on behalf of all the sorrowful, to Jesus in Agony for all who are in agony; to the wearied, trembling, saddened Heart of Jesus for all hearts that are full of weariness, of sadness, of fear, and of bitterness, cannot but attract them: they must come to love it, and to join in it. By the Devotion to the Agonising Heart, the sorrows of Jesus give solace to ths sorrows of man; the grief of man seeks its consolation in the grief of Jesus. We cannot remember Jerusalem without remembering the Agony and the Death of our Consoler and Saviour; in a little while we shall never think of Jerusalem without thinking of the Heart of Jesus.

Would that the fervour of these two united Devotions might oppose the increasing egotism of the present day! Hearts are narrowed and closed by self-interest. How can they be enlarged and opened? Perchance their great desire to save a relation or friend who is at the gate of death and of eternity, or their desire to procure eternal happiness for the dying, will produce that devotion to the Sacred Heart which may transform their nature. Sensuality has invaded society, and one thing which paves the way for it in pious souls is sentimentality. For when piety becomes sentimental, it becomes sensual, because it ceases to be real and practical, self-denying, and devoted to others. How vague are those books which ought to contain solid doctrine! What indifference and apathy is to be seen in the fulfilment of all duties which require an effort, or involve a victory over natural inclinations! In the exercise of this Devotion we stand between those who died yesterday and those who are to die to-morrow; we learn from our Agonising Saviour, Whose Death is daily and hourly renewed on the altars of the universe, how to die to ourselves, while we pray that His merits may be our salvation and that of the dying. It has a great mission to fulfil in modern society, by making us faithful to duty, spite of all the repugnances of feeling and of sense. There are devout people who enter so little into the mystery of suffering, that they lament and are cast down under the burden of trials, believing them to be a special punishment for their sins. What a gentle and consoling light shines forth for them from the Heart of the good Master, in Agony in Jerusalem, in Agony in the guest-chamber on Mount Sion, in Agony in the Grotto of the Mount of Olives, in Agony on the Cross on Calvary's height, always suffering to expiate the sins of others, to make satisfaction for them, so that the bolts of divine justice may be stayed, and mercy may still be shown to a guilty world! The very name of Jerusalem, the Devotion to the Agonising Heart, ought to raise the courage of these afflicted and desponding souls, by teaching them that their sufferings, like those of Jesus, are a gain to the whole world.

All nations will welcome a Devotion coming from Jerusalem, that holy city against which no Christian can have a prejudice. All will find in it a means for the remission of their sins through the tender mercies of our God, whereby the Day-Spring from on high hath visited us, warming the tepid, strengthening the weak, awakening those that sleep, and "enlightening them that sit in darkness and in the shadow of death" (Luke i. 79).

III.—THE COMMUNITY.

CHAPTER I.

CONTEMPLATIVE CONGREGATION OF THE AGONISING HEART.

The work of the Agonising Heart is glorious. Usefulness of the contemplative life. Its principle and its object —love of man and love of God. The more contemplative Orders love God the more they love their neighbours. Contemplative Communities increase devotion and love. This will be specially true of the Community of the Agonising Heart.

THE Heart of Jesus is the Sun of the moral world, and we may apply to It the words of the King of Jerusalem—"The Sun giving light hath looked upon all things, and full of the glory of the Lord is His work" (Ecclus. xlii. 16). It has looked upon the dying, It has looked upon the afflicted; the rays of mercy have fallen upon them and they have glorified the Lord, some by their conversion and others by their resignation. It has looked with special love on some pure souls generous enough to follow the Lamb not only in His joys in Heaven but also in His Agonies on earth. His look has been a ray of light to them in what we call a vocation.

They have united in a Community to pray and to suffer as He did for the salvation of the dying and the consolation of the afflicted. The work is full of the glory of the Lord, and we will give a further account of it.

But in the present day clouds of prejudice obscure the brightness of this glorious work. People ask—What is the use of a contemplative Community? What is the utility of contemplation? How can it promote the salvation of the dying, or give consolation to the afflicted? Let us begin by dispelling this cloud, that the work of the Divine Heart may shine the more brightly and be the better appreciated.

All men who render to their Creator the worship He requires from them may be called religious, but this term is more particularly applied to those who forsake the world and consecrate their whole lives to the service of God. In the same way, as St. Thomas says, the name of "contemplative" is given, not to all those who practise contemplation, but only to those who give up their whole lives to it.* Rachel, sister of Leah and best-beloved of Jacob, and Mary, sister of Martha, "who sat at Jesus' feet and heard His word," are, he adds, types of the contemplative life.† The life of Rachel was not useless to the descendants of Abraham, for she brought forth Joseph, the

* St. Thomas, *Summ.*, ii., 2, q. 81, art. 1, ad. 5.
† *Ibid.*, q. 179, art. 11.

deliverer of his family and the protector of Israel. Nor has the life of Mary Magdalen been useless to the world, for countless penitents have followed in her steps from the depths of sin to the heights of virtue. Can the contemplative life, then, be useless? It is the life of love rather than the exercise of reason.

The contemplative life directs all the powers of the mind to eternal truths, to the mysteries of the Redeemer, but at the same time it fixes all the affections of the heart on God made Man, dwelling ever amongst us, in His mystical Body as well as in the Blessed Sacrament. What is the principle and what is the end of the contemplative life? It is nothing but love. Although the contemplative life, as the Angel of the Schools tells us, essentially belongs to the intelligence, yet its principle is in the affections, because it is love of God that draws us to the contemplation of God. And as the end of anything must correspond with its principle, it follows that the end of the contemplative life must also be found in the affections. We find pleasure in the contemplation of a loved object, and this very pleasure strengthens our love for the object of our contemplation.* Does not the sight of one beloved increase our love? Who is our Beloved? Jesus Christ, at once God and Man, His Humanity as well as His Divinity, the two natures united in that

* St. Thomas, *Summ.*, ii. 2, q. 180, art. vii., ad. 1.

one Person, which are both comprehended in the theological virtue of charity. The contemplation of Jesus Christ, while it inflames the heart with love for the divine nature, must necessarily also kindle love for humanity; therefore the angelic Doctor says—" Love of our neighbour as well as love of God is required for a contemplative life."*

The virginal and faithful Disciple, St. John, who rested on His Master's Bosom, and who had most of the contemplative spirit, was at once the Apostle of charity towards man and charity towards God. He writes : " If any man say, I love God, and hateth his brother, he is a liar. For he that loveth not his brother, whom he seeth, how can he love God, Whom he seeth not? And this commandment we have from God, that he, who loveth God, love also his brother" (1 John iv. 20, 21); and in the same chapter—Every spirit that confesseth not that Jesus Christ is come in the flesh, is not of God (*Ibid.* 3).

If, therefore, contemplative Communities were to deny "that Jesus Christ is come in the flesh," that is to say, to separate His two natures; if they loved the Divinity and were without devotion to the Humanity, their spirit would be that of Antichrist, not that of God. The more the Spirit of God breathes on them the more intense is their charity for their neigh-

* St. Thomas, *Summ.*, ii. 2, q. 180, art. ii., ad. 1.

bour, a charity which embraces all men, because all are united and transfigured in Jesus Christ, all belong to Him, not merely as children to their Father, but as members to their Head. When we look at humanity in some of its poor members, it seems to us contemptible and repulsive, but when we look at it in its glorious Head, the God-Man, we see that it is worthy of all respect, of all love and devotedness. Now, the contemplative life leads us to see Jesus Christ in all men, even in the ignorant whom we try to instruct, and the sinners whom we seek to convert. Diseased and paralysed though they be, they are still members of Jesus Christ; He looks on that which we do for them, for the poor, the afflicted, the sick, the stranger, the captive, as done unto Him. (Matt. xxv. 40.)

The many existing contemplative Communities, whether ancient and austere, like that of Carmel, or modern and less severe, like that of Marie-Réparation, do not merely serve as a counterpoise to the feverish love of activity of the present day, but are themselves the nourishment and the fruit of charity. Their ranks are filled by loving and devoted souls, and they increase love and devotion. Their mortifications, their austerities, and prayers, help the labours of active Communities and make them fruitful. They lead us to the practice of those exercises of piety, which are a necessary and unfailing means of keeping alive our zeal for the salvation of our souls, and our active and compassionate charity for our neighbour. Their example teaches us to renounce ourselves, that we may the better devote ourselves to others, for our devotion to our neighbour will always be in proportion to our renunciation of self. Truly it is needful that some souls should reach the greatest heights of detachment, should forsake themselves, their families, all the goods and pleasures of this world, in order that others may devote themselves generously to the service of Christ's suffering members.

Such advantages are very manifest in the Community of which we are about to give a sketch. What treasures of love must the Agonising Heart of the Saviour have poured into the hearts of women, to enable them to give their fortune, their liberty, their prospects, for the sake of obtaining blessings for the dying! Surely their daily sacrifices must quicken the zeal of all Christians for the conversion of the dying and the consolation of the afflicted. Is it not well that, while the wicked take care to avoid the presence of a Priest on all the great occasions of life, while they bind themselves together in order to die and to make others die in impenitence, some chosen souls should be found who practise devotion to its fullest extent, who draw others on to follow them, and unite them in a holy league, so that all hearts and voices and hands may combine their efforts to save those poor sinners who have but a few moments more to live before their eternal doom is sealed?

We shall satisfy a legitimate curiosity by giving many details regarding this new Congregation. People can become acquainted with active Communities by visiting their houses and conversing with the members; and even the old cloistered and contemplative Communities are known by their history and the lives of their Founders and Saints. But the Community of the Agonising Heart is still in its infancy; it is cloistered, and few of our readers may be able to go to Lyons or to Mende to see it, and then only through a grating. We are obliged to omit many interesting details which relate to persons still living.

CHAPTER II.

IDEA OF THE FOUNDATION.

The Foundress' attraction for Religious life. She is left a widow with ten children; devotes herself to the care of the sick; builds a chapel in honour of the Agonising Heart; wishes to establish a Community; speaks of her desire to Father Lyonnard; and resolves to undertake it.

A YOUNG person who had been brought up very piously, felt from her childhood a great wish to enter the Religious life, but in accordance with the desire of her parents she was married in her seventeenth year. She was always persuaded that God would consider her responsible for her early wishes. This deep but calm conviction interfered in no way with her affection for her husband and children; and it was only a safeguard against evil, and an incentive to good. Her husband, who had been everything she could wish, died the death of the just, on the Feast of the Immaculate Conception, after a very short illness. While she was overwhelmed with sorrow beside his lifeless form, she seemed to see more clearly what God required of her, and she promised to devote the rest of her days to Him.

But arduous duties soon bade her control her grief and restrain her desires; ten children, seven of whom were still minors, required her care. She was obliged to provide for their future, and to look after business matters, which were quite new to her, and caused her many trials during some years. But her promise to God was always before her. What a struggle nature must have gone through in these circumstances? If nature consents to be led to God, it wishes at least to go by a path strewn with roses; but grace leads it to the sacrifice by a painful and thorny road. At the moment when grace calls a person to perform what he or she has long promised and hoped to do, nature will resist—there must be a conflict. The tender mother's heart felt all these difficulties before she tore herself away from her ten children to obey what she considered was the voice of God.

While things were in this state, a friend of hers, who had founded the Hospital of Calvary at Lyons, died, after expressing an earnest desire that she would devote herself to this work. Mdme. ——'s Religious vow was still delayed by business, and she was happy in the meantime to be able to take care of the sick, who had always been dear to her. Her sojourn amongst them was protracted far beyond her expectations; the direction of the establishment was intrusted to her, and six years went by.

At the end of the fourth year another great sorrow came upon her. The bitterness of her desolation drove her one evening, when all were at rest, to pour out her heart at the feet of her good Master; the chapel door was shut, but she knelt outside. She had long had a great devotion to our Saviour's Agony on the Mount of Olives, she had also been in the habit of repeating the prayer to His Agonising Heart, but her devotion to It did not go any further. While she was praying, she promised almost involuntarily to do three things if her trouble was removed. She engaged herself anew to take a vow of evangelical poverty as soon as possible; to perform the exercise of the Hour Sanctified each Thursday night; and to use all her influence to have a chapel built in honour of the Agonising Heart of Jesus. This undertaking seemed little likely to be successful. A great outlay had been made in the hospital before the death of its Foundress, and it was still in debt to a considerable amount, besides which there were a hundred poor people to be supported. And its resources consisted merely in what Providence might please to send through the hands of charitable people. Nevertheless, in a few days the favour which she had asked was granted, and at the end of a year the debt was nearly paid. But how was the chapel to be built? At the beginning of the month of March the sick were invited to pray, that by St. Joseph's intercession the means for the erection of this sanctuary might be provided. By the end of the month, more than ten thousand francs had been given, and the Archbishop allowed the works to begin. Providence furnished the necessary funds, which exceeded one hundred thousand francs. Early in 1859 His Eminence Cardinal Bonald dedicated it to the Agonising Heart.

A little later in the same year, one day just after the Elevation at Mass, the sudden thought darted through Mdme. ——'s mind : " There is an Association in honour of the Agonising Heart of Jesus, why is there not also a Religious Order devoted to Its honour and to the salvation of the dying." It was more than a mere light or direction; it was an impulse which urged her irresistibly forward. It took possession of the pious widow. In vain did she try to treat it as a mere delusion of the imagination, it came back and back again to her mind, and she felt she must write to the Founder of the Association.

Mdme. —— had seen Father Lyonnard only once, at Chambery, at the College of the Society of Jesus, where he was Professor of the class which precedes the rhetorical one, and one of her sons was his pupil. But she was quite unacquainted with him, and had not even noticed his name or appearance. About a year before, on hearing from another member of the Society that the first chapel in honour of the Agonising Heart was about to be built at Lyons, he had written to congratulate her on her good work, and to beg her to take advantage of the opportunity to establish the Confraternity there. She had answered this letter courteously, but had told him plainly that it was impossible to fulfil his desire, as the position of the chapel was not central, and so many other Confraternities already occupied the ground that even the Fathers of the Society thought the Confraternity of the Agonising Heart would have little or no chance of success. She felt some diffidence in writing again to the same person to propose the foundation of a Community under the same title, and with the same object.

But even if her project should be looked

upon as the offspring of an excited imagination, what harm would be done? It would merely be a humiliation, and is not a humiliation a gain to a Christian soul? She therefore wrote to Father Lyonnard, modestly telling him her idea. Her object was simply to obey what she believed to be an inspiration of grace, and when she had sent her letter her heart felt lighter; she had no personal feeling in the matter, and it did not dwell on her mind. In a fortnight Father Lyonnard replied, telling her that she was not the first person who had thought of such a foundation, and begging her to write more fully to him on the subject. She was much struck by his answer, and began to see that God might be about to ask of her a great sacrifice. When she wrote to Father Lyonnard, she begged him to pray that God would make His will known to her.

It was necessary to come to a decision; her term of office as Superioress was nearly at an end, and it was possible that she might not be re-elected. It would cost her much to leave the sick, whom she loved with the heart of a mother; to go far from her own dear children, and into a climate which she knew was unfavourable to her health. But when God asks a sacrifice from us, though He may allow us to weigh and measure its depth and its extent, He does not allow us to hesitate. The sacrifice was one which she had not foreseen, and she almost shrank from it. Her wish had been to obey, to join herself to some other person who would become the Foundress of the new Congregation; she had not supposed that she would have to rule and to take upon herself all the apparent responsibility. If she could have foreseen all this, she would never have made the first step. A worthy follower of St. Ignatius, whom she consulted, told her that it was not fitting that a creature, by want of generosity, should oppose the designs of God, and that by the endeavour to avoid one responsibility, she would incur a far greater one. She bowed her head, and submitted to her cross without investigating the nature of it.

CHAPTER III.

EXECUTION OF THE PROJECT.

The first vocation. Departure for Mende. Token of the divine pleasure by a miraculous cure. Opening of the Novitiate. Death of the first Choir Sister. The Foundress and two Sisters take their vows. Paternal care of Providence. The House at Lyons.

MGR. FOULQUIER, Bishop of Mende, had given permission for the new Foundation to be made in his episcopal city, where Father Lyonnard was then living. He had also written a most kind and encouraging letter in answer to one which the pious widow had addressed to him.

But how could Mdme. —— set off alone to found a Community? To say nothing of the Lay Sisters, at least one Choir Sister was needed to make a beginning; how could such a one be found without letting the secret get abroad? Providence again interposed. A young lady, Louisa ——, wished to devote herself to the Religious life, and was at this moment making a Retreat with the Benedictines before deciding what Order she would enter; the last day found her still uncertain, and she wished to consult her Director. He was the very Religious who had encouraged the Foundress to persevere, and had said to her: "I know a young lady who might perhaps join you. She is at present making a Retreat. I will pray the Agonising Heart of Jesus that if such be His will for her He will send her to me to-morrow." She came, and as she often said since, the proposition made by her Director was like a bright star, pointing out to her the will of God; from that moment her uncertainties and hesitations ceased. On the 14th of September, 1859, Louisa —— and a Lay Sister joined the Foundress at a place she had appointed—it was the celebrated Sanctuary of Fourvières, the first three Nuns of the Agonising Heart of Jesus wished to meet at Mary's feet. The 15th of October, St. Teresa's Feast, was fixed for their final departure. In the morning they had the happiness of hearing the Holy Mass, and of receiving Communion together; and in the evening they were at Puy, a town which Mary loves.

We do not attempt to describe the grief of Mdme. ——'s children. On both sides there is a wound which can never be closed, and which we cannot venture to touch. The poor mother was strengthened to bear nature's weakness by the hope that our Lord would render to them what she was doing for His sake. Her desire to ensure and to increase their eternal happiness made the temporal separation less bitter; and they have since done all that in them lay to bring their mother's Community nearer their home.

The Sunday was spent at Puy, that the projected work might be placed anew under the protection of the Blessed Virgin, who was already acknowledged as the Superior of the Order. On the 17th, in the evening, the travellers arrived at Mende. Everything connected with the foundation had been kept perfectly quiet, and until the day when the Blessed Sacrament was exposed in the chapel, and the Bishop himself spoke of it, nothing was known by the outer world. All the proceedings were marked by Christian prudence, and even before coming to any decision, Father Lyonnard had begged that God would work a miraculous cure as a token of His good pleasure. Augustine ——, the subject of this cure, led a holy life, but for ten years her health had been seriously impaired. The spine seemed to be affected, her stomach was only able to bear very little food, for a year she had been unable even to eat bread, and her weakness was extreme. Most of her time was spent on her bed, or in an arm-chair, and in order to make the effort of getting across the room, or to a chapel close at hand for Communion, she required help, and it generally caused her an increase of suffering. In the month of July, 1859, Augustine heard of the proposed foundation, and felt the importance and interest of its object. She was urged to ask for restoration to health by the intercession of St. Ignatius, but she refused. It was not till the month of September that, fearing lest she was not conforming to the will of God, she made up her mind to join a novena in honour of the compassionate Heart of Mary. It was begun on the Feast of the Seven Dolours of our Lady, and was offered to obtain her recovery, if such was the will of God. She said the *Stabat Mater* and the invocation to the Agonising Heart daily for this intention. But she feared recovery almost as much as she desired it, for she had a strong presentiment of the sacrifices which God would require of her if He restored her to health. Mdme. —— was invited to join in these prayers, and the cure was asked from our Lord as a sign of His intending the establishment of the new Congregation. The pious Foundress went to the Sanctuary at Fourvières, prayed, and had Mass said there.

Some days afterwards a letter informed her that God had granted the desired favour. The sick person had suffered unusually during the novena, on the last day, however, she had been brought into the Church. While Mass was going on, she felt a sort of agitation through her whole body, and she required assistance in going up to the altar. But after receiving Communion, she rose and went back alone to her place, and returned home without any support, to the great surprise of her whole family. In the afternoon she was able to walk without any assistance to the parish church, which stands in the high part of the town, and is difficult of access. No traces of her former sufferings remained save a slight weakness. A few days later Augustine went to Mende, and in the middle of October, within a month after her recovery, she was the first to welcome the future Nuns of the Agonising Heart on their arrival.

Two devout ladies had consented to let their house to the infant Community, and by their kind care a provisional chapel had been prepared. The person who had been miraculously cured assisted them in their preparations; she was able to mount a ladder, and hang curtains, to go downstairs, and remain a long time on her knees, with as much ease as if she had never been ill. Six months afterwards her family sent a doctor, under whose care she had been, to see her, and he was thunderstruck to find her so completely restored.

It was a great happiness to Mdme. —— and the two Sisters who accompanied her from Lyons, to find an altar and a tabernacle in their new abode; to live under the same roof as our Lord, is living under paternal protection, for is it not being close to One Who is Father, Brother, Husband, and Mother? Their good Master did not indeed as yet inhabit His sanctuary, but they were soon to have the blessing of His presence. The day after his arrival, the Bishop of Mende received the Foundress and the Choir Sister with very great kindness, and willingly granted their first request. He promised to celebrate Mass in the new chapel on the following day, October the 19th, the Feast of St. Peter of Alcantara, and he gave them permission to have the Adorable Sacrament always there, on condition that they should keep their Divine Guest company, never leaving the house except to go to confession. The holy Bishop gave an address at Mass, taking for his text the words: " Blessed are they that come in the name of the Lord!" Some Priests and some other persons were present. The abridged formulary of the Institute, which we shall give in the next chapter, was then read, the Bishop declared the Postulate opened, and foretold that this grain of mustard-seed would become a great tree.

In a few weeks the proprietors left the house, and the Postulants were left alone there, and began to make all the arrangements necessary for a cloistered Community. Bad weather delayed the completion of the work until the end of Lent. On the 26th of March, on which day the Feast of the Annunciation was celebrated in 1860, the Bishop blessed the chapel and placed the Blessed Sacrament there. Three days later, on the Feast of the Compassion of our Lady, he gave the Religious dress to the Foundress, to the Choir Sister who had come with her, to Augustine, and to two Lay Sisters. His Lordship then blessed the House, declared the Community cloistered, and opened the Novitiate.

Louisa, the Choir Sister, who had come from Lyons to begin the work, died on the 9th of August, 1861, after three days' illness. Her fervour, her devotion to the cause, and her talent for music, made her loss very deeply felt. The Novice met death with the greatest calmness and resignation, and fell asleep peacefully in the Lord. Her mortal remains were laid out in the choir in her Religious dress, the curtains of the grating were opened, and many came to pray for the departed soul. The funeral was performed with the simplicity suited to her state of Religious humility. A large number of the

Faithful came to honour this wise virgin, who had sacrificed herself for the sake of the dying. One of the Vicars-General and the Parish Priest also assisted, and a neighbouring Community sent sixteen young girls to carry the poor stranger to her grave.

On the 30th of March, 1862, the Feast of our Lady of Compassion, the venerable Bishop received the perpetual vows of the Foundress and of a Choir Sister, the subject of the miracle, as well as the first vows of a Lay Sister.

We cannot detail the many different ways in which the paternal care of Providence has supplied the wants of this little family. One instance must suffice. In 1860 the Community dedicated the month of March to St. Joseph, praying this kind protector of Religious Houses to give them the means of defraying the expenses incurred by the arrangement of the chapel and other indispensable works. At the end of the month, a person who was about to devote herself to God at La Trappe of Montélimar, came to the aid of the poor Community. The Agonising Heart of Jesus had granted her father the grace of a holy death, and she wished to show her gratitude by assisting those Religious who had chosen It as their special object of worship. Ever since a little lamp has been burning every Wednesday before the statue of St. Joseph. His protection has been unfailing. This humble Community, with no resources save the bounty of Providence and the dowries of some Sisters, lives and prospers under the care of our Heavenly Father, Who clothes the lilies of the field and feeds the birds of the air.

Early in the year 1865, a small band of the Nuns being left at Mende to guard the cradle of their Congregations, the others took up their abode in a place situated on the outskirts of La Guillotière and of Lyons. They reached Lyons on the 22nd of February. The next day they went to Fourvières, to commend their new House to the maternal care of our Lady, and on the 24th their Lord and Master came to dwell among them in a temporary chapel. The large and beautiful enclosure surrounding the convent, the calm and solitude of the situation, and the salubrity of the air, make cloistered life more easy to those whose health is delicate. The permanent chapel was blessed on the 22nd of December, 1865. It is simple, and well fitted for devotion. The choir is calculated for at least thirty Religious, and the nave is open to the Faithful.

CHAPTER IV.

ABRIDGED FORMULARY OF THE INSTITUTE.

Object, vows, cloistering, prayer, mortification, work, dowry, auxiliaries, spirit, devotion. Apostolic object often set before the Religious. Prayers for the direction of the intention. This Community meets present needs. It will maintain the Devotion and the Confraternity.

WE give the Rule of the new Institute, which was read publicly in the presence of the Bishop of Mende, at the opening of the Postulation on the 19th of October, 1859 :—

CONTEMPLATIVE CONGREGATION OF RELIGIOUS WOMEN, UNDER THE TITLE OF THE AGONISING HEART OF JESUS.

I. Their object is, by a life of prayer and daily self-sacrifice in honour of, and in union with, the Sacred Heart of Jesus Agonising in the Garden of Olives, to promote the salvation of those who die each day. The number of those who die each day is above 80,000! How many of them need that holy souls should offer themselves voluntarily to God as victims for their salvation?

II. After two years' Novitiate they take the three perpetual Religious vows of poverty, chastity, and obedience, adding one peculiar to the new Congregation, viz., to offer themselves daily to God as victims for those who die each day. Without making any vow on the subject, the Religious of the Agonising Heart will pray much for the Church and for the Sovereign Pontiff.

III. The Order will be cloistered, all relations with the external world being strictly forbidden, but the Religious may go from one Monastery to another when the Superior-General sees fit to send them. The general administration will be in common, and there will be a common Novitiate, from which the Novices will be sent to different Communities.

IV. Their principal occupation will be mental and vocal prayer, and reciting the Psalms of the daily services. If the number of Religious be sufficient, there will be constant intercession for those who die each day, every Religious taking her turn, for a given time, in presence of the Blessed Sacrament.

V. They will add mortification to prayer, not with all the austerity of the Carmelites, but with a moderation which may suit constitutions of no great vigour, while, at the same time, it satisfies the requirements of a life of immolation. Spiritual mortification will be largely practised, by means of exercises of humiliation, public confession of breaches of rule, &c.

VI. In the hours devoted to manual work, a preference will be given to such occupations as making or repairing vestments and altar linen, &c., especially for the benefit of poor churches, according to the means of the Community.

VII. Only persons of suitable education can be admitted as Choir Sisters, and, as a general rule, they must be able to contribute either a dowry, varying in different places from six to eight thousand francs, or the annual interest of that sum. Widows can be admitted if they possess the necessary qualifications.

VIII. Pious persons living in the world will be connected with the Order as Auxiliaries, and will visit and assist the dying. These Auxiliaries will hold communication only with the Superior, or some grave Religious appointed to converse with them. They are not a necessary element, but merely complemental to the Community. Nevertheless, as their cooperation may be very valuable in promoting the glory of God and the welfare of souls, they should be associated, if possible, to every House of the Order.

IX. The spirit of the new Congregation is to be, by the help of God, a happy combination of that of St.

Teresa and that of St. Ignatius. An ardent desire to promote God's glory by contributing to the salvation of souls, especially of the dying, will be joined to a great love of meditation, of prayer, and of sacrifice.

Devotion to the Sacred Person of our Lord Jesus Christ, especially to His Agonising Heart, will be one of the chief characteristics of the new Congregation. The Religious will seek to please their good Master by imitating His virtues, more particularly His humility and gentleness. Their motto will be His words— "Learn of Me, because I am meek and humble of heart." *Discite a Me, qui mitis sum et humilis corde.* (Matt. xi. 29.)

This formulary is explicit, and we will only add a few reflections as to the very Apostolic object of the new Institute.

This object is constantly placed before the Religious. The eleventh of their Common Rules has these words :—"We are bound to offer to God for the salvation of the dying, especially for the dying of every day, the recitation of the daily Divine Services, the intercession made from nine to ten in the evening, the prayer, "O most merciful Jesus," at least once a day, the Advent fast, the Friday discipline, the weekly confession, the exercise of the Five Wounds, and the exercises of reparation. Instead of the daily Divine Service, the Lay Sisters will say two Chaplets and the Office of our Lady of Seven Dolours every day. Choir Sisters who, on account of their age or infirmities, cannot go through the daily Divine Service, will do the same as the Lay Sisters. On

Monday all will hear Holy Mass for those who are to die during the week."

The prayers which every Religious is recommended to use in directing her intention have the same purpose. We give them for the reader's edification :—

"Most holy and most merciful Father, I humbly beseech Thee to accept my intention of performing this day all the works prescribed by my vow of sacrifice, for Thy glory and for the salvation of the dying, especially for those who are to die this day. Grant me Thy blessing, and the light and strength and love I need to fulfil my holy engagements with perfect fidelity, and to bear my cross courageously till death, following the example of Jesus, my God, my King, and my Captain, to Whom, with Thee, in the unity of the Holy Spirit, be glory and love throughout all ages. Amen."

"O my God, I unite my heart and mind to the intentions which the Sacred Hearts of Jesus and Mary had during Their mortal lives, in all that They did and suffered for Thy glory and for the salvation of souls. I wish to have no other object in anything but Thy good pleasure and the fulfilment of Thy holy will. I renounce every other intention. I offer to Thee, in order to obtain the grace of conversion for all the sinners who are to die to-day, the prayers, merits, and sufferings of the Agonising Heart of Jesus and of the compassionate Heart of

Mary, and also the prayers, sufferings, and merits of all the just, both living and dead, especially of the members of our little Congregation, and all the supplications which will be offered Thee to-day in the name of our holy Mother the Church. For this intention I unite myself to the Holy Sacrifices to be offered to-day in all churches throughout the world, and I offer Thee the Holy Victim in union with all Priests who are to offer It to Thee to-day. Amen."

It will be seen that the new Institute is in harmony with the present needs of the Church, and that it also harmonises with the vocation of many souls for a contemplative life. Those who have not physical strength for all the severities of the cloister, and are nevertheless called to this holy state, will find everything they want among the Religious of the Agonising Heart of Jesus, and will also be able to follow the Apostolic impulse, which exerts so great an influence over so many souls in the present day, and sweetens sacrifice by showing its fruit. Every House of the new Order will be like a focus of charity, whence rays of zeal for the salvation of the dying will be always diverging.

The Devotion and the Confraternity of the Agonising Heart will also be guarded, perpetuated, and more widely disseminated. Experience shows us that, too often, a lapse of time brings weakness or even complete extinction to the most approved Devotions and Confraternities. But when the Rule of the Agonising Heart is established in several monasteries, its continuance will be guaranteed far more strongly than that of a simple Association of Christians could possibly be. Now, as one part of its spirit and object is to promote the Devotion to the Agonising Heart of Jesus, and to establish Confraternities in the different churches of the Community, they will last as long as the Order lasts. And, on the other hand, Confraternities will help the Order, as it will certainly be recruited from among their members. In this way charity to the dying will spread more and more widely, supplications and sacrifices will be multiplied for the greater glory of God and the eternal happiness of men.

CHAPTER V.

THE VOW OF IMMOLATION.

Its obligations. Offering of life. God has often accepted this kind of offering. Value of this vow. Resemblance which it produces between Jesus Christ and the Religious. Its power for good.

A PECULIARITY of the new Institution is the vow of immolation by which the Religious offer themselves as a sacrifice to God the Father, in union with the Agonising Heart of Jesus, for the salvation of the dying. It binds the person who pronounces it to the daily offering of her life, a daily quarter of an hour's intercession, the Hour Sanctified in the night between Thursday and Friday, and a weekly fast.

The offering or oblation of life must be sincere; and must be made in words, unless in case of illness. It is enough to say, "My God, I offer Thee my life for the dying;" but the Nuns are accustomed to use the following form: "Almighty and Eternal God, although I am quite unworthy to appear before Thee, yet trusting in Thine infinite goodness, I humbly offer myself as a victim to Thy Divine Majesty, in honour of, and in union with, the Agonising Heart of Thy dear Son Jesus. Dispose of my life, my prayers, and my sufferings, as Thou seest fit, for the salvation of the dying, especially for those who are to die this day. Amen."

God has often accepted the offering of one person's life for that of another. In Communities it has often happened that one Religious has offered to die that another might recover, and God has granted his desire; the first has died at once, contrary to the expectation of all, and the other has been restored to perfect health for many years. People living in the world have also offered their lives for Monks and Nuns, and God has accepted the sacrifice. A daughter has been known to ask as a favour from God that she might die and that a parent, whose life was necessary to her brothers' and sisters' welfare, might be spared; God has consented to the exchange, He has called her to Himself, and the parent has been left to watch over the young children. Must not the offering which the Religious of the Agonising Heart make every day, be always pleasing to our Lord, and be sometimes accepted by Him? It is made not merely to save others from temporal death, but from the fearful misery of eternal death, from the loss of both body and soul in hell. Each morning they say, with an earnest desire to be heard: "O Lord, I trust that I shall live and die in Thy favour; but Thou knowest some who are in danger of dying in sin, perhaps even this very day, unless Thou dost grant them some special grace. I offer to Thee, in order to gain the efficacious grace of conversion for a sinner, the greatest sacrifice I can offer—that of my life. Let my body die, and save this soul!"

By making the vows of poverty, chastity, and obedience, a person gives something real to God; he binds himself to give effect to this poverty, chastity, and obedience. The immolation we speak of is not merely a simple wish of self-sacrifice, but by their vow the Nuns commit themselves entirely to God, that He may take their lives that very moment if He sees fit to do so. Is not this devotedness equivalent to the act of generosity made by a person who offers to die the sooner in order to save the life of another? If anything could be added to the value of this devotedness by making a selection of the individual in whose favour it is made, the Nuns could choose from among the dying who have been specially commended to them, or from some class or condition which particularly interests them. Why should they not do for the dying, what we do for the departed? We do not content ourselves with praying or making some sacrifice for the holy souls in Purgatory in general, but we desire to assist the one most destitute of help, the one nearest to or furthest from Heaven, the one who was most distinguished by a certain virtue or most devoted to some special object. In making or renewing the vow of immolation, might not the Nuns vary their intention, and, while they offer it for the dying in general, apply it particularly to some sinner for whom charity urges them to endeavour to turn the scale?

It may be said that our Saviour Himself made a vow of immolation. When He came into the world He offered Himself to die for sinners, and He renewed this offering in the Garden of Olives. On the morrow God accepted it, and He died on Calvary to save us all. When Nuns of the Agonising Heart enter the Community, they have made up their minds to die for the eternal salvation of sinners, they make a

P

vow of immolation when they enter the long and painful agony of cloister life, and they often renew this vow. Who knows when the morrow may come for them? The morrow of the Passion, of Calvary, of suffering and ignominy, of death for the salvation of dying sinners. That morrow is known to none save God alone; but surely, in His foreknowledge and His providence, He has determined the days or months or years by which He will shorten the life of each Nun in consequence of her vow, or, at least, the increase of anguish and bitterness, of pain and agony, which He will portion out to her throughout her whole life, to enable her to carry into execution her heroic purpose of charity.

What is the work of Jesus each morning on the altar? He sacrifices Himself; but it is by a moral sacrifice, since, as St. Paul tells us, "Christ rising again from the dead, dieth now no more" (Rom. vi. 9). Yet this mystical death avails to unite the Sacrifice of the Altar to the Sacrifice of the Cross, and brings down on the world inestimable graces. The Nuns of the Agonising Heart begin at the altar and end at the Cross. They sacrifice themselves morally with Jesus on the altar; they die mystically, longing with all the fervour of their love to die really with Jesus on the Cross, even by a cruel death, if so be God would accept their sacrifice for a greater number of dying sinners. The

Mount of Olives lies between Mount Sion, where Jesus sacrificed Himself mystically by the institution of the Most Holy Eucharist, and the Hill of Golgotha, where He sacrificed Himself really by an agonising death. The Nuns of the Agonising Heart of Jesus begin by leaving the guest-chamber, the altar where they received their vocation, and where they constantly revive their fervour. Every Religious Community is like a garden; but theirs is the Garden of Olives, whence their prayers and sufferings, their austerities and agonies, bring the oil of grace to the dying. By-and-bye, it may be, they will go and die on Calvary, offering themselves up to the Divine Justice that the guilty may be spared. Can anything have more power with God to gain irresistible grace for hardened sinners, than the cry of these generous souls who offer themselves up every day to the most cruel death—a cry which rises every morning from a whole Commuuity, calling for vengeance to fall, not on others, but on themselves; a cry which is the voice of the Spouses of Christ, kneeling before the altar to receive His precious Body, and uniting their prayer to His Prayer, their agony to His Agony!

This complete sacrifice of a whole Congregation, made every day in union with that of Jesus, is one of the most efficacious means of stemming the torrent of impiety which threatens us. An age of selfishness can only be saved by the spirit of sacrifice; an age of dissipation and carelessness by the spirit of meditation and prayer. The Nuns of the Agonising Heart unite self-sacrifice with separation from the world, and their vow of immolation renewed every day forms in them the habit of that perfect love of which our Saviour speaks—"This is My commandment, that you love one another, as I have loved you. Greater love than this no man hath, that a man lay down his life for his friends" (John xv. 12, 13). The Faithful know this, they reckon on the charity of these fervent Nuns, they eagerly recommend to them the dying whom they love. They say to them: "Oh, you who are bound by a vow to immolate yourselves for the souls of the dying, offer yourselves for my father, or my mother, for my son, my brother, or husband; for this soul, near and dear to me, which is soon to appear before the Sovereign Judge. If my prayer is joined to your sacrifice, it will surely obtain mercy and pardon."

CHAPTER VI.

THE CONSTITUTIONS.

Object of the vocation. Spirit of the Institute. Cloistering. Postulate. First Novitiate. Second Novitiate. Form of Profession. Question of conscience.

THE object of the vocation of these Nuns is, in the first place, to pay a special worship of adoration and love, compassion and reparation, to the Sacred Heart of Jesus, suffering for our salvation throughout the whole course of His mortal life, but above all in the Garden of Olives; and secondly, to offer themselves each day as a victim to God the Father, in union with the Agonising Heart of His Divine Son, to obtain by daily prayer and sacrifice the efficacious grace of a good death for all who are dying throughout the whole world.

We quote some words addressed to the Nuns by their wise Founder, with a view of making known the spirit of the new Institute: "Be thoroughly persuaded that if you would render to the Heart of Jesus the homage that He asks of you, you must make no reservations in your sacrifice—His sacrifice of Himself for you was made without any—devotedness can be repaid only by devotion. Give yourselves entirely to Jesus Christ, for He has condescended to give Himself entirely to you. And as Jesus Christ had to suffer to redeem mankind, make up your minds that in order to attain the end of your vocation—that is, the salvation of the dying—it is necessary for you to be united by prayer and sacrifice with Jesus, the great Mediator and Victim. And as one of the motives which led you to enter the Congregation was to repair the outrages and the ingratitude by which men, especially the dying, have wounded the Agonising Heart of Jesus, let your whole life be a prayer, a holocaust, a constant and honourable reparation offered to that Divine Heart to obtain mercy for them. Have constantly before your mind the remembrance of Him Who, being God, humbled Himself for the love of us, so as to become Man and to die a Victim for our sins. Let your constant study be, with the aid of His grace, to imitate His virtues, especially His gentleness and His humility."

The Institutes of the Order forbid the Nuns to take any part in active life, or even to go into the town. They are allowed to look after the chapel at those hours when it is closed to the public. There are double gratings in the choir and the parlour, with a curtain inside. This is opened in the parlour, as in the Monasteries of the Visitation, and in the choir for the ceremonies, and is so arranged that the tabernacle can always be seen. No one can enter the cloistered part unless for very important reasons, and with the Bishop's permission. No relation or friend, not even a father or mother, can be allowed to come into the monastery to visit a sick or dying Sister, whether she be a Professed Nun, a Novice, or a Postulant. Nor can the Nuns leave their Houses for the recovery of their health.

Before a Postulant is admitted into the interior of the monastery she generally makes a Retreat of three or four days in a place reserved for the purpose. The usual length of the Postulate is three months for Choir Sisters, if they are under forty years of age, and five months if they are older; and for Lay Sisters eight months. The Postulants observe the same Rule as the Novices, and live in the same part of the monastery, but in separate cells or dormitories.

Postulants about to be admitted to the Novitiate prepare for the solemn ceremony of taking the Religious dress by a Retreat of some days. During the Novitiate, they are instructed in the Institutes, Rules, and Customs of the Order, that they may practise them faithfully. They go through the Spiritual Exercises of St. Ignatius for a month, the first half a short time before they take the Religious dress, and the second before they become Professed Nuns.

After a Novitiate of two full years from the time of taking the Religious dress, the Novices, both the Lay and the Choir Sisters, who are approved by their Superiors, become Professed Nuns. The Choir Sisters make perpetual vows of poverty, chastity, and obedience, and a temporary vow for eight years of sacrificing themselves to the dying. The Lay Sisters make temporary vows of poverty, chastity, obedience, and sacrifice for one year; after which, if they prove worthy, they are allowed to make perpetual vows of poverty, chastity, and obedience, and a temporary vow of sacrifice for eight years. After their Profession, the Novices remain under the direction of the Mistress, the Choir Sisters for five years, and the Lay Sisters for one. They keep the Novices' Rule, with some modifications, and are called Novices of the black veil. At the end of the second Novitiate, they are admitted into the number of the Professed, and observe their Rule. Choir Sisters do not take the title of Mother till after they have taken the vow of perpetual immolation.

We give the form of Profession:—" I, Sister Mary N., although most unworthy to appear before God, yet trusting in His infinite goodness, and desirous to honour the Agonising Heart of Jesus in the sufferings of His mortal life, especially in His Agony in the Garden of Olives, make my Profession in this Religious Congregation established in His honour, and in it consecrate myself to God and to the Agonising Heart of His Divine Son Jesus, in the sight of His glorious Mother, the Immaculate Virgin Mary, of all the company of Heaven, and all here present, by these perpetual vows of poverty, chastity, and obedience, and by the temporary vow of immolation for the salvation of those who die each day, in conformity with the Institutes and Rules of the said Congregation. I bind myself, according to the same Institute, to the strict observance of being cloistered, and I promise to honour the compassionate Heart of Mary, to pray often for the Sovereign Pontiff, for the Church, for the conversion of heretics, and for my Sisters in this Order. Amen."

In reading these Institutes we cannot fail to observe in every page the traces of a mind experienced in the Priesthood and in Religious life, and well acquainted with Communities of women, and the abuses which may arise in them. We will merely draw attention to one most important point, to what is called the report of the conscience.

The Saints have always looked on this as one of the most important means of advancing in virtue, and of maintaining a family spirit in Communities. On the part of the inferior it implies simplicity, humility, and confidence; on the part of the superior, charity, prudence, discretion, and often an amount of knowledge greater than that required by a Confessor. How many Priests would be unable to give adequate direction to some of those whose confessions they hear! How then should a woman, without the study of dogmatic or moral theology, without the knowledge requisite for a Confessor, have light sufficient to direct a soul in matters which are most delicate. Therefore the Church, while giving an unreserved sanction to the report of conscience in all cases where the Religious Superior is a Priest, imposes certain restrictions where that office is filled by a woman. The Roman Court has often declared that under such circumstances the report of conscience is confined to public breaches of the Rule, and to progress in all the virtues : " Manifestatio conscientiæ restringitur quoad publicas transgressiones regulæ, et ad progressum in virtutibus."

What is laid down by the Institutes of the Agonising Heart? " The spirit of the Church, as regards the report of conscience, is that you should act with entire liberty, and without constraint, merely telling the faults you have committed against the Rule, and your progress in all the virtues, reserving all other matters for the ear of your Confessor or Director. The matter of the report of conscience commonly made to the Mother Superior consists of those things which it is necessary for her to know, in order to be able to direct you in the faithful observance of your Rule, and in your progress in perfection."

CHAPTER VII.

A DAY.

The cell. The Religious dress. Act of offering. Psalmody. Mass. Manual labour. Meals. Recreation. Rosary. Intercession. Homage to the Dying Saviour's Agony.

WE think many of our readers will like to have some further details as to the Profession and daily life of a Nun of the Agonising Heart.

The House which we visited at Mende does not belong to the Community, but is merely rented by the year. It is small and unpretending in appearance, and everything inside bespeaks an extreme poverty, in accordance with the lowly beginnings of the work. Order and cleanliness reign throughout, but it has not been possible to make all the arrangements desirable for a Community. The cells are, in general, very narrow, cold, and low; their furniture consists of a straw mattress, a chair, a small table, and a picture. The Nun spends the night and some hours of the day in her cell. She rises at five o'clock, and begins her hour of mental prayer at half-past five.

Her dress may be thus described:—A full brown gown, with wide, long sleeves, a girdle of red cord with knots, one end of which on the right side reaches the ground, at the left side a black rosary of large beads, with a large cross and medal of the Agonising Heart. Above the dress a large long white scapulary bound with red. It is white in honour of our Lady of Seven Dolours, and on the breast is a great red Heart, surrounded by the crown of thorns, and surmounted by the cross and flames; on one side is the lance piercing it, and on the other is placed the sponge; beneath are the three nails, made, like the Heart, out of red cloth. For the head, white bands and a large black veil. During the ceremonies in the choir a long black cloak is worn. The Nun wears a large crucifix over her heart, but hidden by the scapulary, and on the fourth finger of the right hand a gold ring, with these words engraved inside— "Through Mary, Jesus; His Heart and His Cross." The Lay Sister wears a silver ring, which does not open and has no motto. The ring is the symbol of that charity which should unite the Nun to her Divine Spouse, in spite of crosses and thorns, of the lance and nails, of gall and of bitterness. Is she not pledged to remain faithful to Him in suffering and in death? This union is often brought before her mind, and she makes the following offering of herself every day :—

"O my Creator and Sovereign Master, behold at Thy Feet a most unworthy victim, who offers herself most humbly to Thy Divine Majesty, as a sacrifice of expiation and reparation for the salvation of poor dying souls. But I am burdened with the weight of my own sins—how can I venture to implore Thy mercy for so many souls on the brink of eternity? If I were alone in my prayer and my attempt at reparation, I should be full of fear, but I have with me and on my side the Agonising Heart of Thy most dear Son Jesus. I unite my prayer to His Prayer in the Garden of Olives, my sacrifice to His Sacrifice on the Cross. Therefore, in union with this adorable Victim, I draw near to Thee, O my God, trusting that in Thine infinite goodness Thou wilt condescend to hear me. O my God, would that I were able, by the help of Thy grace, after the example and by the intercession of Thy glorious Apostle St. Paul, 'to supply that which is wanting of the sufferings of Christ,' and, by my sufferings and my immolation, to take part with Him in His work of reparation! Holy Father, let Thine anger be turned away. Let the voice of the Blood of Jesus, Thy beloved Son, let the groans and sighs of His Agonising Heart come before the Throne of Thine infinite mercy, and obtain for me, Thy most unworthy servant, and for my Sisters, abundant sanctifying graces, and for those who are to die to-day and to-morrow the gift of pardon and eternal salvation. Amen."

After their mental prayer, the Nuns begin Divine Service. They sing it also at eleven, at three, and at six. The Psalms are sung gravely, and in a monotone—neither slow nor hurried — with their united voices and with much devotion. On Feasts the Service is sung rather more slowly and solemnly than on other days. In the presence of the Blessed Sacrament the attitude of the Nuns is that of profound veneration. The impression conveyed to the mind by hearing them is that they are full of earnestness, and that, in the ardour of their faith and love, they aspire to unite their hearts to the Sacred Heart of Jesus praising His Heavenly Father, with Mary, and the choirs of Angels and the whole company of Heaven.

At seven o'clock they hear Holy Mass. Immediately after the Elevation, each one makes privately, in conformity with their vow of immolation, this offering of her life : " Almighty and Eternal God, although I am quite unworthy to appear before Thee, yet trusting in Thine infinite goodness, I most humbly offer myself as a victim to Thy Divine Majesty, in honour of, and in union with, the Agonising Heart of Thy beloved Son Jesus. Be pleased to dispose of my life, of my prayers, and my sufferings, according to Thy good pleasure, for the salvation of the dying, especially of those who are to die this day. Amen."

On Friday, this offering is made aloud, and in common. The Nuns thus participate in one of the principal acts of their Agonising Saviour—the oblation of His life to God His

Father, and His acceptance of suffering and of death.

At a quarter past eight, at ten, at a quarter to two, and at half-past three, the Nuns occupy themselves in manual work, either in the Community-room or in their cells. The Choir Sisters do needlework and the necessary work of the house. They also undertake work for people living in the world, but not of a kind that merely ministers to vanity. Their chosen occupations are those which minister to the worship of God, such as making flowers, vestments, and linen for churches, and altar-bread.

Dinner is at noon, and supper at seven o'clock. Their diet is that of the middling classes of society, except in cases of illness; it is the same for all. Their Rule allows the use of meat, at dinner only, on Sunday, Monday, Tuesday, and Thursday, at the other meals on these days they practise abstinence, as well as at all meals on Wednesday, Friday, and Saturday. They do not avail themselves of the dispensations commonly given in some dioceses in regard to the Saturday abstinence and certain days in Lent. Besides the weekly fast, which they make on Saturday, they fast every week-day during Advent, except the Feast of the Immaculate Conception.

There is recreation for an hour after dinner, and for three quarters of an hour after supper. The first Friday in each month, all Fridays in

Lent, and the vigils of certain Feasts, are spent in silence. On other days their recreation time is spent together, and in the same place; all the Sisters are bound to be present, and about the middle there is a moment of silence, during which all place themselves in the presence of God, and in union with Him. The recreation is marked by gaiety and cheerfulness, and they generally employ themselves in some light work. An amiable simplicity which generally distinguishes these Sisters tends to give a pleasing tone of domestic life.

At half-past one they go to the chapel and say the Rosary together; on Friday it is the Rosary of the Seven Dolours. This Rosary was first adopted by the seven holy Founders of the Order of Servants of Mary. It has seven divisions, each consisting of a *Pater noster* and seven *Ave Marias*, and three *Ave Marias* are said at the end. The Sovereign Pontiff has attached numerous indulgences to its recitation.

At half-past two all the Nuns meet together before the Blessed Sacrament, to make half an hour's intercession for the dying of the day, and especially for those who are dying at that very time. When the Community is sufficiently numerous, this intercession is kept up all through the day, each Sister taking half an hour in turn.

At three o'clock the bell rings, and all prostrate themselves in honour of the Agony of

THE COMMUNITY. 185

Jesus dying on Calvary. They remain prostrate as long as the bell continues to ring; then, with their arms stretched out in the form of a cross, they say the prayer, "O most merciful Jesus," &c. On Friday, before this prayer, they repeat the words of our Lord upon the Cross. In certain churches a pious custom, handed down to us from ages of faith, still exists: a bell, called the Agony bell, is rung in honour of the dying Saviour. At Angoulême, and some other cathedrals, the great bell tolls seven strokes on Friday. Would not the general restoration of this custom be an excellent protest against the blasphemies which in the present day are uttered against the divinity of our Saviour? At least it would be a homage of reparation. In a Brief, *Ad passionis*, dated the 23rd of September, 1740, Benedict XIV. expressed his desire that all the Faithful should kneel down on Friday about three o'clock in the afternoon, and say five *Paters* and five *Aves*, in honour of the Agony and Death of our Lord Jesus Christ. He granted for every time this should be done, an indulgence of one hundred days, which was afterwards confirmed by Gregory XVI. in a Decree of the 24th of September, 1838.

At a quarter past nine the Nuns go to bed, but two or three of them continue till ten o'clock in prayer for those who are to die during the night; each one takes her turn in this intercession. All perform the Devotion of the

Holy Hour, from eleven o'clock till midnight on Thursday night, but their hours are then altered, so as to give the same amount of sleep.

CHAPTER VIII.

A PROFESSION.

St. Agnes model of all virgins who consecrate themselves to the Lord. Preface sung by the Celebrant. Words sung by the virgins. Special observance at the Profession in honour of the Agony of our Lord. Peculiarities in the ceremony of giving the Religious dress.

THE Profession of the Sisters of the Agonising Heart takes place during Mass, and is made with all the ceremonies prescribed in the Service of the Roman Pontifical for the benediction and consecration of virgins.

One touching peculiarity is that the words sung by the Sister on taking the vow are those pronounced by St. Agnes, a martyr to virginity and to faith, who was put to death at the age of thirteen, on the 21st of January, 305. The son of the Governor of Rome wished to marry her, but she answered him—"Do you think that I can ever forsake my Bridegroom, to Whom I am so closely united that my soul lives only by His love, nor that you have any merit to enable you to appear as His rival? For He is possessed of six qualities, which make Him beyond all others worthy of love; He is noble, beautiful, wise, rich, good, and powerful. If you would know Who He is, He has for His Father, God, Who begot Him without any mother, and the Mother who brought Him forth into the world was ever a Virgin. His beauty so far surpasses the splendour of the sun and moon and all the stars that it inspires the very company of Heaven with admiration, and they confess in silence that, in comparison with Him, they are but darkness. He is so wise, and has so held me captive by His love, that I can think of no other, and now, while I speak of His perfection, I am so happy that, although your presence is horrible to me, yet I am glad to see you, that I may speak of Him. He is so rich that He has given me treasures worth all the Roman Empire, and all who serve Him are laden with good things. What shall I say of His goodness, which is beyond all measure? To show it the more, He has marked me with His Blood. He has pledged His Word to me that He will never forsake me. He has taken me for His Spouse, He has given me beautiful garments and most precious jewels. He is so powerful that all the powers of Heaven and earth cannot conquer Him. The sick are healed by His touch, and His voice recals the dead to life.

"Therefore I am wholly His; I love Him more than my soul and my life, and I would gladly die for Him. Loving Him, I am chaste; coming into His presence, I am pure; embracing Him, I am a virgin. Is it likely that I should leave Him for the hope of any recompense, or for fear of any suffering?"

The Governor of Rome threatened to have the innocent child taken to a haunt of infamy. "I fear nothing," said she, "for with me is an Angel, one of the countless servants of my Bridegroom; he guards me, and will wonderfully defend me. My Jesus, Whom you know not, surrounds me on all sides like an impregnable wall."

The Governor's brutal threat was executed, but the virgin was preserved from all stain. She was thrown into the fire, but the flames did not touch her, and she exclaimed: "O Almighty God, worthy of all praise and honour, I laud and magnify Thy Holy Name. By the virtue of Thine only Son, Jesus Christ, I have overcome the violence of tyrants, and passed unharmed through the abode of impurity. And now, to add to these wonders, I feel that Thy celestial Spirit tempers the heat of the fire, and makes the flame pleasant and the heat agreeable to me, while my persecutors feel its power. Blessed be Thy Holy Name, O Lord, for now I see what I desired, I enjoy what I hoped for, I possess Him Whom I loved. Let my heart and tongue, my soul, and all that is within me bless and glorify Thee. I am coming to Thee, the true and eternal God, Who reignest with Thine only Son Jesus Christ throughout all ages. Amen."

Agnes was martyred by the sword, and buried outside the walls. Her parents came constantly to pray at her grave, and eight days after her martyrdom she appeared to them in the midst of a great multitude of Virgins, all clothed in robes of cloth of gold adorned with precious stones, and crowned with flowers, pearls, and diamonds. The glorious and triumphant Saint had by her side a lamb more white than snow. She stood still, made her companions stand before her father and mother, and said to them: " Dearest parents, do not weep for me as dead, but rather rejoice with me that I have won a crown of glory in Heaven, amongst this holy company; rejoice that I possess Him Whom, during my earthly life, I loved with all my heart and soul."

The Church, which, on the 21st of January, celebrates Agnes' love of virginity, even unto martyrdom, celebrates also, on the 28th of the same month, the consoling apparition of the dear child to her family. Such is the model which she places before Christian virgins in the solemn moment of their consecration to the Lord. She puts the words of Agnes into their mouths, that her spirit may be in their hearts. She would say to them: " Be faithful to your Divine Bridegroom even unto death; love virginity more than life; but also, even in the midst of the Religious life, where you are always close to the Lamb of God in the Blessed Sacrament, honour your father and mother, console them in a separation which has cost their hearts so much, and when they come to visit you in your mystic tomb, appear before them radiant with joy, full of respect and overflowing with love." We will not here enter into all the details of the Service of the Roman Pontifical, but will merely express our regret that the ceremonial is not, in some Communities, performed with greater exactness.

How full of instruction is the Preface which the Celebrant sings. Virginity is placed above marriage, because, while despising its pleasure, it seeks for that union with God of which marriage is a figure. Virginity should be accompanied by a prudent modesty, a wise benignity, a grave sweetness, a chaste liberty, an ardent love of God, a blameless life which seeks no praise, purity of soul, filial fear, a habit of seeking and finding all in the Divine Spouse of souls. O Lord, be Thou the honour and joy of virgins, their consolation in sadness, their counsel in perplexity, their defence against injustice, their patience in tribulation, their riches in poverty, their food in time of dearth, and their healing in infirmity.

How striking is the sight of all these virgins prostrated on the ground during the Litanies of the Saints which precede the Preface. How it touches a Christian heart to hear them sing the words of St. Agatha, Virgin and Martyr—" I am the servant of Christ, and therefore I show my lowly condition;" and then those of St. Agnes —" He has set His mark upon my face, that I may admit no other lover. I am espoused to Him Whom the Angels serve, and Whose beauty the sun and moon admire. He has given me a ring as the pledge of His truth, and adorned me with a crown as His Spouse. He has put on me a long robe of gold and a costly chain. And now I see that which I desired, I possess what I hoped for; I am united in Heaven to Him Whom on earth I loved entirely. I have inhaled the honey and milk on His lips, and His Blood dyes my cheeks." Before the end of the ceremony, the Bishop or the Celebrant pronounces anathema and malediction against any one who should make the Spouses of Christ forsake the banner of chastity and the service of God.

Every Nun is to be led to the altar by her god-mothers, who are elderly ladies, and, if possible, her relations. These god-mothers only appear at the taking of the Religious dress, and the first were the ladies who formed the council of the Association at Mende. During the ceremonial of Profession, reference is made to the special vocation of honouring the Agonies of Jesus, and of praying for the dying. The Litanies of the Agonising are said while the Nuns about to make their Profession remain bowed down. Kneeling in the middle of the choir, they chant in a slow voice—"Father, if Thou wilt, remove this chalice from me, but yet not my will, but Thine, be done." Then coming near the grating, and again kneeling, they chant —"Father, forgive them, for they know not what they do." The Superior silently presents a great crucifix; they kiss it, and then each Nun says—"Father, into Thy hands I commend my spirit." At the end of the Mass several tapers are lighted around the statue of Mary, and when the Priest has finished the last Gospel, one of the Nuns standing close to the statue, chants slowly and devoutly—*Ecce Mater tua.* "Behold thy Mother." Then the Nuns just received turn towards her, and bend one knee to the ground. They are led by the Superior, and come with their crowns in their hands, and, after making a lowly reverence, lay them at the feet of Mary, while the choir chant or sing—*Ecce filius tuus.* "Behold thy child." The new Nuns then take a crown of thorns from behind the statue, and place it on their heads instead of the crown of roses, and, again bowing down, depart.

Some similar peculiarities are observed on taking the Religious dress. The Postulant is led by her god-mother to the grating, and, kneeling there, kisses the five wounds of a crucifix presented by the Superior. While the Superior holds it, the Postulant takes it in both hands, and before kissing it says—"My crucified Jesus, I choose Thee for my portion." She rises, and after she has respectfully embraced her god-mother, the Superior opens the door of the Nuns' choir and lets her in. After she has put on her Religious dress and received her name, she turns to the statue of Mary, kneels down, bends low, gets up, and kisses her feet. She then kisses the Superior's hand and embraces her Sisters, saying to each—" Pray for me."

CHAPTER IX.

DIFFERENT REPRESENTATIONS OF THE AGONY OF JESUS.

The new Institute represents the Saviour's Agony. Material representation. Historical representation. Moral representation.

YET more must be said to make our readers thoroughly acquainted with the new Order; we must show them how it attains its double purpose of honouring the Agony of Jesus and contributing to the salvation of the dying. Our concluding chapters will be devoted to these subjects.

The Saviour of the world has been pleased to come and make His abode amongst us on earth until the end of time. He dwells with us not merely by His real presence in the Sacrament of His Love, but also by His mystical

R

presence in the Church, which is His Body, and in the Faithful, who are His members. If every real Christian is another Christ, far more is the Catholic Church, consisting of the Faithful and their lawful Pastors, the continuation of the life of Jesus Christ on earth. But by virtue of their vocation, the Religious Orders are peculiarly bound to represent the mysteries of our Saviour's life. Every Institute is the reproduction of one phase of His adorable life, and a special honour to some special mystery. The Agony of Jesus was not yet represented by any special Religious family, and the Community of the Agonising Heart came to fill up this void.

The physical representation is the least important, although the material images which appeal to the senses are intended to produce a spiritual and sanctifying impression on the soul. By the constitution of the new Institute, all its churches are to be dedicated to the Agonising Heart, and are to have above the high altar a picture of our Lord praying in the Garden of Olives. Medals and pictures of the same mystery are much used in the monasteries. At Mende, a grotto has been built in the garden in remembrance of the Grotto of the Agony; our Lord is represented praying, while an Angel descending from Heaven offers Him the bitter chalice; the Nuns often come here to share their Master's sorrows, and we ourselves have had the happiness of praying on the same spot.

Near at hand is a fountain of water, which serves for the garden. It seemed to us a symbol of the effects of our Lord's Agony, and of the life of these fervent Nuns. Like poor withering plants in the garden of the Church, we should all perish hopelessly if our Divine Saviour's tears, and drops of Blood, had not filled the fountain of mercy; that fountain still receives the tears, and sighs, and prayers of His faithful Spouses, the innocent and mortified companions of Jesus in His Agony. It remains for us, the Priests of the Lord, to come and draw from its depths grace and pardon for sinners and the dying, that they may bring forth fruits of salvation, pleasing to God.

The historical representation of the Agonising Heart of the God-Man, becomes more and more manifest throughout the whole Church. The Body, like its Head, has had a hidden life and a glorious life, a life of action and one of suffering. Is it not now passing through an agony, not the agony of death, for it can never die, but an agony of fear, of heaviness and sadness, an agony which makes the august representative of Jesus Christ weep, while those alas! who had promised to watch with him and defend him are sleeping. But many faithful souls are suffering with him, are seeking to share his sorrows and soften his afflictions. They were born too late to bear Jesus company on the Mount of Olives, so they endeavour, as some compensation, to become angels of consolation to His Vicar in the Holy See. They show their respect and love, they make the sacrifice of their possessions, they devote themselves to defend the right and soothe the anguish of the Pontiff King.

In the very year that our common Father suffered so cruelly, this new Order arose, whose mission is to lighten the sorrows of the Church and of its visible and its invisible Head by sharing them. What will be the fate of the infant Congregation? We cannot say, but we may be sure that suffering, and even agony, will be its portion, for, like many other Religious Orders, it will not escape blame, or reproach, or persecution.

The moral representation of the Saviour's Agony is found every day in souls. The Agonising Heart of Jesus, by the force of Its love, draws all suffering hearts to Itself. What heart has not sometimes suffered agonies? Which of us can escape them? Our Saviour's Agony arose from four principal causes, which may in turn oppress our hearts. These causes were: His coming Passion, the rage of the devil, the sight of all the sins of the world, and compassion for all the sufferings of humanity. Even should we escape personal suffering, or the direct attacks of the devil, we cannot, if we follow the path of virtue, escape the agony of penitence or the agony of compassion. The more pure and fervent we are, the more we love God and our neighbours, the more acutely shall we feel the outrages offered to Him, and the evils they suffer; and therefore the nearer shall we approach to that moral agony. Was there ever a Saint who did not long to suffer agony with Jesus? In the present day an increasing number of hearts share the Agony of the Divine Spouse of souls, and by their perfect resignation console Him for all the injuries which He receives from the careless and the profane.

If the Agonies of Jesus are multiplied, so are also the angels of consolation. To console Him is the object of the societies of reparation which are established amongst us. Is not this also the aim of the souls who consecrate themselves to God in honour of the Agonising Heart? The more pure they are, the more do they love God. No doubt, when God accepts their sacrifice He multiplies their sufferings, that they may become more like the image of His first-born Son, and may offer up acts of adoration corresponding to the ever-renewed outrages of men.

Providence is sometimes pleased to choose from the very ranks of great sinners, those who are to make amends for the outrages of others, so that an honourable reparation may be offered by the blasphemers themselves. We are bound closely together in the order of grace, as well as in the order of nature, and if it is well for us to have soldiers who make their breasts a rampart against our enemies, it is better still to have these holy victims, who bear all sacrifices, and expose themselves to all kinds of suffering, in order to make some amends for the outrages committed against God's honour, and to obtain grace for their brethren. Thus, one of the most sinning parts of our generation has offered an expiation, and the age which has caused so much Agony to the God-Man, has produced the Nuns of the Agonising Heart.

The mystical representation still remains to be developed; it consists of different exercises performed by the Community, with the view of recalling the sad mystery of the Garden of Olives.

CHAPTER X.

MYSTICAL REPRESENTATION.

Exercise of the Five Wounds. Exercises of reparation. The Holy Hour. Oblation — Intercession — Fast. Humiliation in the refectory. Prayer to the Angel of Consolation.

PENITENTIAL exercises have their appointed place in the daily life of a Nun of the Agonising Heart, and they tend to perfect her resemblance to Jesus Christ, as well in that which He had to suffer in order to enter into His glory, as in that which He had to undergo in order to save us. The Chapter is concluded by an exercise of fraternal correction, practised in honour of the Five Wounds of our Lord, especially of the Wound in His Heart, in order to obtain the correction of faults. This is called the Exercise of the Five Wounds; and the Nun who has to undergo it, is admonished by the others of all her external faults against the Rules and the Institutes.

The exercises of reparation promote both zeal and penitence; for their object is to make amends for the outrages which the dying have throughout the whole course of their lives offered to the Agonising Heart of Jesus, and also to obtain for each one of them the grace of a good death.

The exercises of reparation are annual, monthly, weekly, and daily. The annual is performed on Good Friday in honour of the Passion of the Son of God; the monthly on the first Friday of the month; the weekly also generally on Friday. At each one of these exercises special prayers are made for all who are to die before its recurrence. We give a detailed account only of those exercises which mystically represent the Agony of Jesus.

At a little before eleven o'clock each Thursday night, the Sister whose office it is, wakens the others for the Holy Hour. She calls them in the words of our Lord—" Watch and pray," and they rise immediately, answering—" Let us watch and pray." They go to the choir, and at an appointed signal they enter the church, two and two, and take their places in front of the tabernacle. At the first stroke of eleven, all bow down to receive the blessing of our Lord, and to offer Him this holy exercise. They rise up, and one of the Sisters reads aloud the account of our Saviour's Agony in the Garden of Olives given in the Gospels. At the words, "And going a little further, He fell upon His face," all kneel down and prostrate themselves, uniting their prayer to His Prayer, their sacrifice to His Sacrifice, and offering themselves in union with Him as victims to His Father. At the words, "And when He arose up from prayer and was come to His Disciples," they rise. The very words spoken by Jesus in His Agony are repeated, first by the Superior and then by the Sisters all together in a slow voice. They kiss the ground, and continue on their knees, praying, till a quarter before twelve. Then the Superior, accompanied by two of the Nuns, goes with lighted candles and kneels on the ground, straight before the altar; she says aloud the act of reparation to the Agonising Heart of Jesus, and some other prayers. As midnight strikes, all bow down to receive the blessing of Jesus from the tabernacle, and then they retire.

The Community honours and represents the Agony of our Divine Master in many other ways. The three things included in the vow of immolation all recal His Agony. The daily offering of life answers to that made by our Saviour in the Garden of Olives, when He accepted the death which His Father willed He should undergo for our salvation. The daily intercession corresponds to the prolonged Prayer of His Agony; and the weekly fast recals the physical exhaustion occasioned by His Bloody Sweat.

A mortification in honour of the same mystery is practised in the refectory. The Sister who has been allowed to humble herself after the example of her Agonising Saviour, kneels in the middle of the refectory, with her head bent down and her hands joined, and says: "O my God, behold I come to do Thy holy will. I belong to Thee, I am Thy victim, do with me as it shall seem good to Thee. I accept in a spirit of reparation, and in union with my Saviour in the Garden of Olives, the humiliation which Thou art pleased to bestow upon me; mercifully strengthen my weakness, and pardon my many sins." She then prostrates herself on the ground and says, after a short pause: "My Father, if it be possible, let this chalice pass from me; nevertheless, not as I will, but as Thou wilt." The Superior reproves her for her faults. Then prostrating herself again, she says: "My Father, if this chalice may not pass away, but I must drink it, Thy will be done," and mentally renews the sacrifice of herself for those in their last agony. She afterwards leaves the refectory and goes to pray for the dying before the Blessed Sacrament.

Let me ask those who live in the enjoyment of the pleasures of this world, and accuse contemplative Orders of idleness and uselessness, whether there is anything in all their feasts and gatherings so noble, so generous, or so useful to human nature as this representation of the Agony of the Son of God, made by humble women during the hours that they spend in banqueting and sleeping, who offer their lives as a sacrifice in order to save those who die each day? While you are sleeping on your soft pillows, or seeking pleasures in scenes of gaiety, where your heart's best feelings are squandered, and where perhaps Christian modesty is little regarded, these angels of the earth are watching and praying to obtain mercy for our dying brethren. Perhaps your whole life on earth will prove to be less useful than one hour that they have thus spent.

These innocent souls cannot forget the Angel who consoled Jesus in His Agony, for their most earnest longing is, after the example of that heavenly spirit, to console their Divine Master. It is natural that they should have a special Devotion in his honour; and they are in the habit of using the following prayer:—

"O my Saviour Jesus, Who, because of

Thine immense love for men, didst consent to endure a sadness even unto death, in the Garden of Olives, and Who in Thy great weakness and Agony didst not disdain to be upheld and strengthened by an Angel, do not reject the consolation which Thy most unworthy servant desires to offer Thee with all possible veneration and love. Alas! my most kind Saviour, I have had a share in causing Thine Agony. For my sake, Thou hast suffered, Thou hast poured forth a sweat of blood, Thou hast shed many tears, Thou hast sighed and groaned. O my Jesus, I have united my prayer to Thy Prayer, and my sacrifice to Thy Sacrifice, to expiate my sins, and to save the souls of the dying; let me now, in order to console Thee, be in spirit with the Angel of the Agony. Let me abide with Thee in the lonely Grotto, that I may watch Thy sorrows, that I may grieve with Thee, and drain that bitter chalice to the dregs which Thy Heavenly Father has given Thee to drink.

"Glorious Minister of the Most High, to whom was intrusted the sublime mission of consoling and strengthening thy God, let me remain with thee at my Saviour's side. Would that I also could bring Him some solace in the mortal Agony of His loving Heart! Give me strength and courage and love like thine, that I may pray and suffer, and die with Jesus! Amen."

The devotion of the Nuns of the Agonising Heart to the compassionate Heart of the Virgin Mother, will easily be understood when we remember that, of all human creatures, Mary alone participated in His Agony.

CHAPTER XI.

DEVOTION TO THE COMPASSIONATE HEART OF MARY.

Honours paid to the Blessed Virgin. Daily prayer. Consecration made on Saturday. Exercises of humiliation on her seven principal Feasts. Zeal of Mary for the salvation of the agonising. Let us imitate this zeal.

THE Blessed Disciple St. John, who, so shortly before his Master's Agony, rested on His Divine Heart, is one of the patrons of the new Order, but it is more especially devoted to our Blessed Lady. We have spoken elsewhere of the agony which Mary underwent during the Agony of Jesus,* and have shown that her compassion and her grief reached their highest pitch in that awful hour.

It is the intention of the Nuns of the Agonising Heart to have in each of their churches a chapel dedicated to the compassionate Heart

* *L'Agonie de Jésus*, liv. xii., ch. vi., t. iii., pp. 532—544.

of Mary. They are in the habit of invoking this tender Mother, and recalling to her memory the sorrows she endured. The Feast of her Seven Dolours on the third Sunday in September, that of her Compassion on Friday in Passion Week, and that of the Sacred Heart of Mary, are celebrated with great solemnity. The most holy Virgin is considered as the Superior of the whole Congregation and of each monastery; her statue is enthroned in the choir between the places of the Mother Superior and the Mother Assistant. Two gilt keys, representing the keys of the house, are placed at her feet. Her statue occupies the place of honour in the refectory and in all the Community-rooms. Each Nun has a little figure of Mary in her cell, with a wooden crucifix. Every morning the work of the day is distributed in her name—this is called the obedience of Mary. Every night, before they retire, the Sisters bow before her statue and kiss her feet. In the morning, on rising, each one asks her blessing privately, kneeling and saying—*Nos cum prole pia, benedicat Virgo Maria.* "May the Virgin Mary, with her loving Child, bless us." Recreation is opened by an *Ave Maria.*

The following invocations to the Heart of Mary and the Heart of Jesus are frequently used : "Compassionate Heart of Mary, help poor sinners;" "Agonising Heart of Jesus, have pity on the dying."

We give a prayer, which the Sisters say at least twice a day:—

"O most merciful Mary, Refuge of Sinners, I pray thee, by the sorrows of thy compassionate Heart, and by the death of thy well-beloved Son Jesus, obtain the grace of a true conversion for all sinners in the world, especially for those who lead others astray by bad example or pernicious doctrine. Beseech God to remember His former mercies, and to send this evil generation some Apostolic men, mighty in deed and word, some great Saints, endued with strength from on high, to revive faith amongst Catholic nations, and to stem the torrent of threatened calamities. Amen."

On Friday, all who can, join those Sisters who are making their intercession from nine to ten o'clock in the evening, and honour Mary in her desolation by mental or vocal prayer.

On Saturday the act of consecration is made: "Holy Virgin, Mother of Dolours, we consecrate ourselves to thine Immaculate Heart. Remember that Jesus gave us to thee on Calvary; show thyself our Mother, sweetest Mary. We intrust to thy care all our temporal and eternal interests, particularly the government of our Congregation, beseeching thee to animate all those who enter it with thine own spirit. Bless us, dear Mother, and grant that, like thee, we may in all things only seek the good pleasure of God and His greater glory. Amen."

On the seven principal Feasts of the Blessed Virgin an exercise of humiliation is made by the Nuns, with the three-fold object of rendering homage to the Dolours of the Mother of God; of gaining, by the merits of those sufferings, an increase of the spirit of their vocation, that is to say, of the spirit of prayer and sacrifice, of gentleness and humility, of zeal for souls, of devotion to the Sacred Person of our Lord, and compassion for His Agonies; and lastly, of obtaining graces of conversion and salvation for the dying, for heretics, and sinners. Perpetual supplication to the compassionate Heart of Mary for the present needs of the Church was established at Mende, on the 29th of September, 1865.

These practices of devotion keep in view not only the compassion of the Virgin Mother for the Agony of her Divine Son, but also the zeal of Mary for the salvation of the dying.

In a revelation made to the Abbess of Agréda regarding the fearful dangers which beset the dying, the Blessed Virgin said: "I will not tell you how many of the dying are lost, for you, who love God, would die of grief if you knew their number. But if you would help those who are in such peril, begin by doing all you can to convince the living that, in order to die a good death, they must take great care of their souls. Never forget to pray for this intention; beg the Almighty to destroy the snares and weapons which the devil brings to bear against the dying, and to put them to flight by His own right hand. You know I used to pray thus for mortals, and I would have you follow my example."*

Though our Lady is now in Heaven, she is still the model of all members of the Confraternity or Congregation of the Agonising in their daily prayers and works for the salvation of the dying. "Worldly friends," says St. Liguori, "are attentive to us while fortune favours us, but when we fall into trouble, and especially when death comes, they turn their backs upon us. But Mary does not treat her servants thus; she is never seen to forsake them in any adversity, far less in the greatest of all, in the agony of death. She is our life while we are still in this place of exile; she is our sweetest comfort at the hour of death, which she makes both calm and happy. Ever since the day that Mary had the mingled sorrow and consolation of helping the Head of all the Elect in His last hours, it has been her privilege to assist all the Elect in their passage to eternity; therefore the Church teaches us to say to her—'Pray for us, poor sinners, now and at the hour of our death.'"

The greatest honour and consolation we can give to the Agonising Heart of Jesus and the

* Marie d'Agréda, *La Cité Mystique*, pt. 2, n. v., ch. xv., nn. 880—884.

compassionate Heart of Mary is by endeavouring to lessen the number of sinners, especially of those who die in sin, for it was the sight of sin and of the torments of the lost that pierced those Sacred Hearts as with a sword. Should not the very thought of the zeal of the Blessed Virgin quicken our zeal? A fervent Religious says:—" When we think of all that Mary had done for each of those souls, those who ceaselessly, momentarily, are causing their own eternal punishment; when we call to mind the many graces which she has obtained for every one of them, and, consequently, the yearning of her maternal heart for their final perseverance and everlasting salvation, we may form some idea how acceptable this particular Devotion must be to her. She has an especial predilection for a death-bed, and she seems to choose it for a remarkable exercise of her jurisdiction. It is there that she so visibly cooperates with Jesus in the redemption of mankind. But she seeks for us to cooperate with her also. She would fain join our hearts to her Heart, our prayers to her prayer. Is she not the one Mother of us all? Are not the dying our brothers and our sisters in the gentle motherhood of Mary? The interests of the human family are at stake, and we must not be indifferent about it. Mary in many mysterious ways helped her Son to die. By His will, and in the satisfaction of her own maternal love, she has now given her aid at the death-bed of many millions. By devout thoughts, by pious practices, by frequent ejaculations, by so many prayers to which the Church has attached indulgences, let us obtain a happy ending for ourselves, by following Mary everywhere to the death-beds she attends."*

CHAPTER XII.

THE SALVATION OF THE AGONISING.

The good that women can do by a hidden life. A cloistered Nun has sometimes been chosen by God to cooperate with an Apostolic man. Usefulness of the Nuns of the Agonising Heart, especially to the dying.

How does the new Institute attain its second object, the salvation of the dying? How can Nuns who are always shut up in their cloister benefit the dying?

We must begin by observing, that it is not by a life of outward movement and action, of journeying and preaching, that God wills women to promote the well-being of Christian society; but by their inward life, their hidden virtues, their retirement and prayer, by a constant devotion of self, a silent and unobtrusive devo-

* Faber, *The Foot of the Cross, or, the Sorrows of Mary*, ch. vi.

tion. We borrow some reflections on this subject from one of the old biographers of St. Mary of the Incarnation: "As women, for reasons into which we need not enter, are excluded from public employments, it would seem that the perfection suited to their sex is found in the Christian care of their families. Nevertheless, it sometimes pleases God, for the manifestation of His glory and goodness, to bestow extraordinary gifts on certain humble, pious, modest women, who are free from all ties of earthly affections, and to lead them to perform actions of such public importance, that they are like lamps shining upon the holy candlestick, and like the sun when it rises to the world in the high places of God (Ecclus. xxvi. 21, 22). So Deborah was chosen to give victory and peace to Israel by the wiseness of her counsels and the justice of her judgments. Judith and Esther preserved their people from impending ruin. Again, in the Acts of the Apostles, we see that though they were not permitted to speak in the assemblies of the Faithful, certain holy women were led by their zeal for souls to accompany the Apostles on their journeys, that they might be able to teach the way of salvation in private. Such were Prisca, Mary, and some others, whom St. Paul calls his helpers, who have laboured with him in the Gospel, to whom all the Churches of the Gentiles give thanks, and whose names are in the book of life (Rom. xvi. 3, 6; Phil. iv. 3). Our Lord has been pleased from time to time to renew the wonders of the early ages of His Church, and we may mention Mdlle. Acarie as an instance of one whose apostolic zeal almost equalled that of St. Paul's helpers, and was rewarded by numerous conversions."*

If a married woman, living in her family, was enabled to do much good, is it likely that a consecrated virgin, free from all family cares, and specially devoted to the relief of human misery, will not have equal power over the hearts of the godly by her prayers, and over the hearts of sinners by her works? The history of the Church shows us, that God in His providence has often associated a cloistered Nun with some Saint who was actively engaged in the duties of the Apostolic ministry.

In the introduction of the Cause of the Venerable Mother Agnes, who contributed so largely to the good works done by M. Olier, the following remark is made: "It has often been observed that some very holy women have had a great affection for certain men of eminent sanctity, whom God seemed specially to confide to their care, and that they have constantly assisted them by their counsels. Because of their very ardent zeal for the conversion of

* Boucher, *Histoire de la B. Marie de l'Incarnation*, publiée par Mgr. l'Evêque d'Orleans, l. ii., ch. iii.

sinners, God allowed them to be associated with these eminent men for the furtherance of Apostolic labours which their sex forbade them to undertake in person. They helped them by their prayers, so that the fruits of conversion were due to both. For a real conversion two things are required, that the sinners heart should be touched by the grace of God, and that he should be instructed in his duties. The first of these is obtained by the prayer of these holy women, and the second by the preaching and other labours of Apostolic men. Moreover, the prayers of holy women are also answered by the light God gives to the Priest, and by the opportunities He grants him of bringing more souls to repentance."*

The last biographer of the Founder of St. Sulpice adds : " This union of grace, which tended to raise the servant of God to the highest perfection, and to make him share the zeal of Mother Agnes, is not without an example in the lives of Apostolic men. It is like that formed by the Holy Spirit between St. John of the Cross and St. Teresa, with a view of communicating to the reformer of Carmel the zeal of the seraphic virgin, and making him, by means of her exhortations, a fit instrument to execute the designs of God. The providence of God works in a marvellous manner sometimes, in order to preserve great men from the

* *Vie de M. Olier*, pt. 1, l. iii., note.

poison of pride, which is ready to taint the holiest things; it makes an apparently feeble instrument necessary to their success; it connects the graces of illumination and conversion with the ardent prayer of a simple woman; and grants it an efficacy denied to eloquence or mere human efforts."*

Of what use to the world then are the Nuns of the Agonising Heart of Jesus? Of the same use as all good women, as all holy and devoted souls; ten such would have sufficed to save Sodom, and some few now suffice to draw down the mercy of God on sinners who only deserve His justice. Of what use are they? They are the helpers and supporters, perhaps they even act as a stimulus on the zealous laymen and holy Priests who are labouring in the world to reconcile the dying to Christ. Of what use? They animate our fervour, they excite us to holy emulation by the daily austerities which they choose as their portion, in order that men may have the gifts and graces needed in their ministry to the dying. Of what use? They gain for us opportunities of exerting our zeal, and the means of success in our efforts for the salvation of the dying. Of what use? To keep us humble, for we who speak and act may perhaps one day see with astonishment, that the successes which we attributed to our works were really due to some lowly Spouse of

* Faillon, *Vie de M. Olier*, pt. I, l. iii., n. ix.

Christ who had lived a life of sacrifice and prayer in the cloister. Of what use? To obtain for the dying, by our prayers and our sacrifices, that grace which may transform their hearts, while we, by our words, may remove the dark clouds hanging over their understandings.

If the Nuns of the Agonising Heart do not stand in the breach to fight the battles of our Lord, yet they are silently preparing the way by which souls are to come to repentance, and to escape the worst evils. People often say that there is no need for convents, and that a life of prayer and penance is a useless life. But they might as well say that a physician is enough to heal the sick, and that the laboratory where remedies are prepared is of no use. No, the life that is consumed in the rigours of penance to save the agonising from a terrible end, is far from an idle one, and it will not be in vain for devout Christians, who do not feel themselves called upon to make all the sacrifices of these voluntary victims, at least to join with them as far as they are able. Whether, with them, you choose the Mount of Olives for your dwelling-place, or make it the object of your frequent pilgrimages, your work will be eminently Apostolic in its nature. The career open to your zeal comprises not merely one province or one empire, you have the whole universe for your battle-field, and since your Apostolate extends to all who are to die, every human being is included in your sacrifices and your charity.*

CHAPTER XIII.

PRAYERS OF CONTEMPLATIVE ORDERS.

Detractors of contemplative life inconsistent and unjust. Good done by contemplative Orders. Examples of sinners converted by them. Value of the prayers of a whole Community.

LET us ask those who in the name of universal tolerance anathematise the contemplative life, those who in the name of religious liberty condemn the perpetual worship of God, and those who in the name of humanity claim for the poor and sick the time spent in solitude and prayer, and the alms bestowed on the Spouses of Jesus Christ—What good do you do to the poor and sick? how much time do you devote to them? what portion of your income is spent in lessening their sufferings? when do you honour God? when do you think of your Saviour and of the eternal truths? when do you think of your own death, and of the salvation of your soul? You have anathemas for houses of prayer, but you have none for the haunts of vice! you applaud dancers and

* *Messager du Sacré Cœur*, Novembre, 1861, art. i., n. iii., pp. 187, 188.

actresses, and you speak evil of those sublime women who sacrifice themselves for your sakes! you encourage the opening of a new theatre, you have nothing to say against those places where souls are lost, yet you would fetter the few holy Congregations who seek in silence to expiate the crimes of the world and to obtain salvation for those who are perishing. Hypocrites! who would cast out the mote that you think you see in the existence or in the mode of life of the contemplative Orders, how is it that you do not see and do not cast out the beam from your own eyes and the eyes of your friends—the uselessness of your life, the scandal to which you give rise, and your indifference to the misfortunes of others?

In these days, while so many men are working for the extension of Satan's empire, why should not holy women labour for the spread of the Kingdom of Christ? God is often pleased to choose the weak things of the world to confound the strong; and it may be for His glory to let the simple prayer of a poor woman counteract the evil efforts of rich and learned men. Our century presents no fairer sight to the eye of Faith. Floods of corruption and atheism are spread over the world by the press, and other means; but just as the grains of sand form a barrier against the waves of the ocean, so the mighty designs of the wicked are often brought to nothing by lowly women, who remain quietly where God has placed them, praying, loving, and suffering. Take courage, Christian Mothers! take courage, Spouses of Christ! Make some return to Christianity for what it has done for you. It has given you honour and liberty; give it the souls of the living, even at the last moment rescue them for an eternity of bliss; bring Jesus to the souls of the dying who are stained with sin, as Mary, your model, brought Him into the world which was polluted with iniquity.

Even if the Nuns of the Agonising Heart did nothing but pray for the dying, we might look for many and glorious conversions, for the contemplative life raises some souls to eminent holiness, unites them to God, "Whose ear is open unto their prayer." It is true that all members of the Church are bound to pray for each other, and that this duty is fulfilled in the cloister better than anywhere else, and, moreover, that the power of prayer is, generally speaking, in proportion to the holiness of the person who prays. The law of mediation is considered as universal in the spiritual creation, and the supernatural perfection of any creature gives a greater power of acting on others, and of obtaining for them the grace of God. We have examples of this truth in the lives of many contemplative Nuns, who, although it was not their especial vocation to pray for the dying, succeeded in saving many of them.

St. Victoire Fornari, Foundress of the Annonciades Célestes, wished to have prayers for Preachers made in her monastery during Lent, that they might work earnestly and successfully in gaining souls for God. Having heard that some one had committed a great sin, she was overwhelmed with grief, and bound herself by a vow to fast and perform many penances that the sinner might be enlightened and converted. God heard her prayers, and brought him to repentance. On the 11th of September, 1612, she heard that the soul of a dying person, for whose salvation she had often prayed, was in the greatest danger. She turned immediately with fervent love to God, and said: "Lord, Thou canst not refuse me this soul, for Thou hast promised it to me." She repeated these words many times, extending her arms in the form of a cross. While she was praying, a bright light surrounded her, as if the sun's rays had broken through a cloud. This light lasted about the time it takes to repeat a *Miserere*. Victoire recovered her consciousness, but was so weak that she could not stand. She said that the person was dead, that his soul was saved, but would have to remain long in Purgatory.*

In the life of St. Catharine Ricci, another contemplative Nun, we read the following anecdote: "On the 12th of September, 1542, a

* *Vita della B. Maria Vittoria Fornari*, l. ii., cap. vii.

criminal was condemned to death, and fell into a fearful state of despair, he was tempted to give himself up to Satan, and to blaspheme God, and to wish for eternal damnation. The efforts made by zealous and experienced men to prepare him for death seemed only to increase his obstinacy and fury. This soul was recommended to the prayers of the Saint. She prostrated herself immediately on the ground, determined to die there rather than rise without obtaining her petition. With ardent charity, she exclaimed: 'O Lord, Thou canst take my life, and send me to hell if Thou wilt, for I am Thine, Thou art my absolute Master, but I pray Thee that the soul of the wretched being who is about to be executed may go to Heaven. O my God, I know Thou wilt hear me, I know Thou wilt save this soul!' Our Lord appeared to her with a severe and angry countenance, and told her that this malefactor was extremely obstinate in his wickedness, that he was rejecting light, and that therefore divine justice must take its course. The Saint reminded the Son of God of all that He had suffered for this soul. Our Lord again answered her, taking the side of justice, and Catharine continued to plead for mercy. At length He consented to grant the request of His servant, but only on condition that she should bear some part of the sufferings due to this sinner for his enormous crimes. Immediately, Catharine began to feel fearful pains, which continued for several years. But at the first moment of her sufferings, the sinner's heart began to turn to God. He wept, he expressed a desire to confess his sins, he acknowledged himself worthy of a thousand deaths more terrible than the one before him, and he died with such resignation, patience, and joy, that all who saw him were melted to tears."*

Can the fervent prayers and constant sacrifices of the Nuns of the Agonising Heart of Jesus fail to obtain the conversion of sinners? It is not one soul alone that prays, not even one Religious family, but it is a whole Society animated by the same ideas, directing all its powers to the same end. These numerous prayers must necessarily be of great effect, and in truth, though the Congregation has only existed for a short time, God has already manifested by unequivocal signs the power He vouchsafes to give to this Society for the conversion of the dying.

* Sandrini, *Vita di Santa Caterina de Ricci*, l. ii., cap. vi., n. 2.

CHAPTER XIV.

CONVERSIONS OBTAINED.

Conversion of a merchant at Mende. Conversion of an old man in the diocese of Bordeaux. Holy deaths of the relations of Nuns. To multiply conversions let us promote the extension of the Society.

WE proceed to give some examples of what has already been said. A respectable merchant was living at Mende in 1863. His fortune was considerable, and though he was not yet advanced in years he had retired from active business to enjoy the repose which is so welcome after toil. In the pressure of worldly affairs he had lost sight of eternity, and though he had received a Christian education, forty-two years had now passed since he had approached the sacraments. His brother, a Priest, and his sister, a worthy mother of a family, tried to recal to his mind his early religious impressions, but he always put off the subject till "by-and-bye." Alas! in how many cases that time never comes. Grace constantly knocked at the door, but he continued deaf to the warnings of God and of man. Nevertheless, he could not escape God's mercy.

He went to rest one night in perfect health; in the morning a sudden attack brought him apparently to the point of death. The doctor and the Priest were both summoned, but they had to wait several hours before he recovered consciousness. Fear made him ready to listen to the voice of God's messenger, and he began to make his confession. The Agonising Heart of Jesus had granted him time, in answer to the prayers offered by a Christian family. But as the day went on he felt better, and, in his accustomed spirit of procrastination, he told the Priest that he would soon go to him and finish his confession.

Things continued in this state till the third day of his illness, when a relation went to recommend him to the prayers of her sister, a Nun of the Agonising Heart. The Nun took her medal and gave it to her sister, saying—"Tell him that, as I cannot go to see him, I send him this token of my affection." He received it well, kissed it, and wore it round his neck. Seeing him in such a good frame of mind, the relation went again for the Priest; he made his confession, and received absolution.

Those around him were uncertain whether the last sacraments should be at once administered; the dying man expressed his willingness to abide by their judgment, and only feared lest he was not sufficiently prepared. It was decided that the Holy Viaticum should be given to him, and he was anxious again to purify his conscience, that he might be ready for so great a blessing. After he had received the Bread of Angels his countenance lighted up with joy. He embraced those who had contributed to his happiness and those who had witnessed it. He begged a young Priest, a relation, to remain with him during the night, which he spent in prayer. He made a generous sacrifice of his life to God, and renewed his acts of faith, hope, charity, and contrition. Weakness came on suddenly; his Confessor hastened to his side, and gave him Extreme Unction. The happy penitent was calm and resigned, and responded to all the sentiments suggested to him. He lost the power of speech, but his consciousness remained, and he gave signs of continued peace. He died with the serenity of the just, and went to increase the number of the Elect who owe their eternal salvation to the Agonising Heart of Jesus.*

The conversion of an old man of eighty, in the diocese of Bordeaux, was obtained in the same year by the Nuns. He was of good birth, and distinguished by high moral qualities, but had been led astray by false philosophy. Inconsistently enough, he showed respect for religion, and bore his frequent and tedious sufferings with great resignation, while he continued to live without the sacraments, in which, he said, he had no belief. His age and infirmities made his family feel most anxious about him, but they could gain no other answer to their entreaties.

* *Messager du Sacré Cœur*, Sept., 1863, art. iv., pp. 144—146.

One of his nieces had particularly recommended him to the prayers of the Nuns of the Agonising Heart and of the members of the Confraternity, but for a long time no change was apparent. About the middle of the year 1863, a letter was written to the Nuns, begging them to make a new effort. They sent a little picture of the Agonising Heart, which was placed in the sick man's room, that it might be near him in his agony. Grace prevailed; the Priest was admitted, and, to the great joy of the pious family, was able to accomplish his holy mission. Soon afterwards the old man lost the use of his faculties. He died, leaving those who had watched him full of gratitude to the merciful Agonising Heart, Whose picture had been an instrument of his salvation.*

The world accuses Nuns of forgetting and neglecting their families. Yet often nothing but their prayers and sacrifices could open Heaven to a father, or brother, or uncle, who has spent his whole life far from God. When love becomes supernatural, it gains fresh constancy and power, it obtains grace from Heaven for those who are its objects. It has frequently been observed that the relations of those who have devoted themselves to God in the Religious life have happy deaths. The Nuns of the Agonising Heart cannot but desire, and cannot fail to obtain, the grace of conversion or of final perseverance for

* *Messager du Sacré Cœur*, Sept., 1863, art. iv., p. 147.

the dying members of their families. A letter which the Foundress wrote to us on the 6th of March, 1864, shows that this is the case. How this mother, who left her ten children in the world, must rejoice in the thought that her consecration to the Agonies of the Divine Heart may obtain for all those that are dear to her a calm and happy death. "Recent and consoling facts," she says, "have shown us that the Agonising Heart of Jesus grants special favours to the relations of our Sisters. In one case, an old man rejoiced in the hope that his daughter, a Nun in our Community, would obtain for him the grace of a happy death; and to the last his mind remained unclouded, and he died as a Christian should die. Another instance is that of a man in the full vigour of life, upright and honourable in his conduct, who, though his faith remained unimpaired, neglected his religious duties. He fell ill, and a relation of his who is with us told us of her fears about his soul, and we all united in supplication to the Agonising Heart of Jesus. Very soon the sick man sent for the Priest, that he might make his peace with God, and, through the different phases of a rapid and painful malady, he showed a wonderful degree of resignation and patience. He kissed the crucifix and died, pronouncing the name of Jesus. I think, indeed, that it would wrong the Heart of our good Master to doubt that our devotion to the dying obtains special graces for those whom we have forsaken only for His sake."

If, then, your hearts are grieved at the sight of the multitude of impenitent, dying sinners, if you wish to give for ever to Jesus the souls which He has bought with His Blood, help this new Congregation to extend its branches in all directions. Encourage the spread of this Order, multiply its houses and its members, and you will multiply the means of spiritual assistance for the dying, many of whom would be lost without this special aid. And you, Christian wives and mothers, who would do anything for the eternal welfare of your husbands and children, shrink not from the sacrifice, if our Lord should call one of your daughters to honour His Agonising Heart, and promote the salvation of the dying. She will be a blessed victim, sacrificing herself daily for her family; she will gain the souls of her father and brothers, and she will appear to her mother as an angel of consolation in her hours of greatest suffering.

CHAPTER XV.

THE FUTURE.

Providential designs. The spirit of prayer and contemplation is kept alive amongst us by the contemplative Orders. The Agonising Heart of Jesus will revive it among the active Orders. Perhaps it may become a common centre of prayer for all. The active spiritual life, or mixed life, will be developed; this is the most perfect of all. The work will become a great and fruitful tree.

WE cannot conclude this work without some reflections as to the future. It is not given to us, indeed, to draw aside the veil, yet Providence seems to let hope shine through it. For why did God call this Devotion of the Agonising Heart into being towards the middle of this century? Why, twelve years later, Devotion to the Holy Agony? What is the reason of the rapid growth of these two Devotions? Why have they produced, not only Confraternities but Religious Congregations, whose principle object is contemplation and prayer? No doubt a purpose of Providence is here; a plan has been made of which we only see the beginning. We know not when it will reach perfection, but we cannot doubt that great things are in preparation.

As the fever of action gains on modern society, as the whirl of material progress carries it on, an increasing need arises for the preservation of that spirit of retirement, of prayer and of sacrifice, which ensures moral progress and the eternal salvation of souls. Now, one of the means which God employs to keep it alive is the presence of the contemplative Orders, which He has restored amongst us, and which tend by their example to quicken the fervour of Christians living in the world. The Carmelites, the Trappistines, the Carthusians, already render us this great service, and the Nuns of the Agonising Heart are about to do the same.

Even active Religious Orders are in great danger of losing the spirit of fervent and inward devotion in an age which has lost faith in the supernatural, and which has, alas! witnessed so many defections. Without any change in the letter and spirit of their Institutes, would it not be well if some means could be found whereby to preserve the inward and supernatural spirit of devotion, which is the very essence of their vitality? And would not devotion to the Agonising Heart of the God-Man, if introduced into Religious Houses under the form of perpetual intercession, tend to accomplish this object? And if a great centre of prayers and sacrifices could be established, to which, in virtue of the Communion of Saints, active Communities might be joined, on conditions consistent with their Institutes, would not still greater good be the result? For this centre, being full of the spirit of prayer and sacrifice, which belongs to the Agonising Heart of our Lord, would constantly keep it alive amongst them.

By the grace of God this may be done. But this centre or focus ought to be surrounded by the most favourable circumstances for the maintenance and increase of the supernatural and inward spirit of devotion. Everything that could tend to impair that spirit ought to be kept at a distance, since the object is to assist Congregations which are already exposed to this peril. If the central body were itself likely to lose that spirit, it would have enough to do to keep it alive among its own members. In many Monastic Orders, by the Sovereign Pontiff's desire, there are certain Houses set apart, where those members who are called to a life of more especial contemplation and more profound solitude are able to retire. These Houses draw down a blessing on the active Religious of the Order. Why should not an entire Congregation of women in the same way pray for the many active Orders, and keep alive amongst them, by example, the inward spirit of devotion and of sacrifice ? If there is a bond of union amongst all human beings, if all the Faithful are able to form an Association for doing good, might not all Communities of women be likewise united in their prayers and their sacrifices, so that, while the contemplative pray for the active, the active should work for the contemplative ?

The infant Congregation of the Agonising Heart of Jesus seems to be called by God to perform this office for the active Orders. But, to fulfil such a vocation, it must devote its energies to prayer and sacrifice, that is to say, it must be exclusively contemplative—its action must be confined to the prudent affiliation of people living in the world.

The influence of the Agonising Heart of our Master will also reach Congregations of men. It will diffuse through all pious souls, whether in the world or in the cloister, the supernatural and inward spirit of prayer and immolation, just as the peculiar functions of our hearts is to vivify the whole body. The spirit of prayer and sacrifice which comes from the Agonising Heart will be accompanied by Its own supernatural life. There is nothing more remarkable in our Lord's Agony in the Garden of Olives, than His prolonged Prayer, His voluntary immolation of Himself, His inward spirit of real devotion; for real devotion means entire self-sacrifice—giving oneself up unreservedly to God and to man. And this spirit is often wanting, especially in those who are themselves afflicted, tempted, or in their last agony. They pray little, they sacrifice themselves still less. The dying are but a portion of that barren soil which the Agonising Heart longs to water and to refresh. A beginning has been made where the need was greatest, but further progress will soon be seen, and all souls, in the hour of affliction as well as in the hour of death, will partake of benefits due to the holy and life-giving Agony of Jesus.

With God, with Jesus Himself, contemplation precedes action. So must it be with Religious Orders. The contemplative element is first developed, but the active follows, and the delay only serves to make it the more vigorous and fruitful. The love of God and the love of souls are inseparable, and their united force will make the contemplative Nuns of the Agonising Heart desire that others should act. They will seek fellow-workers, whose visible ministry may apply to the souls of the dying the graces which they have won by their invisible life. And this will be the highest perfection of the work. St. Thomas Aquinas says:—"A life of contemplation is better than that life of mere activity in what concerns the body. But the active life of one who, by preaching and teaching, communicates to others that which he has gained by contemplation, is far more perfect than a purely contemplative life, because it pre-supposes an abundance of contemplation. Therefore our Lord chose for Himself this kind of active life."*

A simple contemplative life, then, ranks higher than a merely active life, such as that of lay people who are engaged in servile occu-

---

* St. Thomas, *Summ.*, pt. 3., q. 40, art. i., ad 2.

pations, or of Religious who devote themselves to the solace of the ills of the body. But it ranks less high than active spiritual life, in which teaching, labours for the conversion of sinners, unbelievers, and the dying, are added to contemplation. This mixed life is the most perfect, the most fruitful, and the most exalted. God contemplates and God acts. He acts internally, and His action is an eternal creation; He acts externally, and His action is a temporal creation. The Son of God, when He became Man, passed from contemplation to action; even in the Garden of Olives, where He contemplated for so long a time, He vouchsafed to act to a certain degree. In the Church, the contemplative Orders were a preparation for the active Orders. The Order of the Agonising Heart, in its tendency to the perfection of a complete conformity to our Lord, will add the active to the contemplative element, and will keep up the spirit of prayer throughout all its ramifications, at the same time devoting some of its members to external labour, in order that more abundant fruits of salvation may thus be brought forth.

This work was the least of all works, a mere grain of mustard-seed, which the God-Man sowed in His field the Church. Already it has grown up, and by-and-bye it will become a great tree, so that the birds of the air may come and dwell in the branches thereof (Matt. xiii. 31, 32).

Throughout the whole tree the life-giving sap of prayer will circulate, and this very sap will make the branches put forth the wholesome fruits of outward activity. The contemplative element will be the trunk and the roots, drawing nourishment from the earth, which was moistened by the Bloody Sweat of the Agonising Saviour, while the active element will be the branches laden with fruit. Its benefits will be visible to all, it will bend over the dying and the afflicted to give them the food they need, protecting some from the fiery rain of avenging justice, and affording to others the refreshing shade which tempers their passing trials.

PRAYERS FOR THE DYING.

I.

DAILY PRAYER.

[Latin.]

O CLEMENTISSIME JESU, amator animarum, obsecro Te per agoniam Cordis Tui Sanctissimi et per dolores Matris Tuæ Immaculatæ, lava in sanguine tuo peccatores totius mundi nunc positos in agonia, et hodie morituros. Amen.

Cor Jesu in agonia factum, miserere morientium.

[English.]

O most merciful Jesus, Lover of Souls, I pray Thee, by the Agony of Thy most Sacred Heart, and by the sorrows of Thy Immaculate Mother, cleanse in Thine own Blood the sinners of the whole world who are now in their agony, and are to die this day. Amen.

Heart of Jesus, once in Agony, pity the dying.*

* There is an indulgence of 100 days every time this prayer is said. A plenary indulgence if it is said three times a day, at distinct intervals, for a month together.

II.

LITANY OF JESUS IN THE GARDEN OF OLIVES.

Lord have mercy.
Christ have mercy.
Lord have mercy.
Christ hear us.
Christ graciously hear us.
God the Father of Heaven, *have mercy on us.*
God the Son, Redeemer of the world, *have mercy on us.*
God the Holy Ghost, *have mercy on us.*
Holy Trinity one God, *have mercy on us.*
Jesus, Who didst go to a solitary place and pray, before delivering Thyself up to Thine enemies, *have mercy on the dying.*
Jesus, Whose Heart was oppressed by mortal sadness in the Garden of Gethsemane, *have mercy on the dying.*
Jesus, filled with fear at the thought of the torments of Thy Passion, and at our sins, *have mercy on the dying.*
Jesus, overwhelmed with sadness by foreseeing the fruitlessness of Thy sufferings for souls which refuse to profit by them, *have mercy on the dying.*
Jesus, strengthened in Thine Agony by an Angel from Heaven, *have mercy on the dying.*
Jesus, accepting the chalice of Thy Passion for love of us, *have mercy on the dying.*
Jesus, Who didst say in the midst of Thine

anguish, "Father, not My will, but Thine be done," *have mercy on the dying.*
Jesus, exhausted by Thy Sweat of Blood, *have mercy on the dying.*
Jesus, persevering in prayer, notwithstanding the weakness of nature, *have mercy on the dying.*
Jesus, Who didst come to Thine Apostles and find them sleeping, *have mercy on the dying.*
Jesus, Who didst say to them, "Could you not watch with Me one hour?" *have mercy on the dying.*
Lamb of God, Who takest away the sins of the world, *spare us, O Lord.*
Lamb of God, Who takest away the sins of the world, *graciously hear us, O Lord.*
Lamb of God, Who takest away the sins of the world, *have mercy upon us, O Lord.*

V. Heart of Jesus, once in Agony,
R. Pity the dying.

Let us pray.

O my Divine Saviour, call to mind the sadness of Heart, and the fear which oppressed Thee, when, being in an Agony, Thou didst pray the longer, and didst water the earth with a Sweat of Blood. I offer it to Thee with tender love, and I beseech Thee, by every drop of that Precious Blood, to have mercy on the dying, and to put away all their sins. Amen.*

---

* Boulangé, *Manuel de la Confrérie du Cœur Agonisant,* erigée en faveur des agonisants de chaque jour, dans la chapelle de la Visitation Sainte Marie, de Mans, pp. 45—47.

III.
LITANY OF ST. JOSEPH.

LORD have mercy.
Christ have mercy.
Lord have mercy.
Christ hear us.
Christ graciously hear us.
God the Father of Heaven, *have mercy on us.*
God the Son, Redeemer of the world, *have mercy on us.*
God the Holy Ghost, *have mercy on us.*
Holy Mary, spouse of St. Joseph, *pray for the dying.*
St. Joseph, virgin spouse of the Immaculate Virgin, *pray for the dying.*
St. Joseph, perfect pattern of all virtue, *pray for the dying.*
St. Joseph, great model of faith and of confidence in God, *pray for the dying.*
St. Joseph, who didst adore the new-born Saviour in the manger, *pray for the dying.*
St. Joseph, who didst see the first drops of His Blood, shed in His Circumcision, *pray for the dying.*
St. Joseph, who with Mary didst offer the Lord in the Temple, for the salvation of the world, *pray for the dying.*
St. Joseph, who, obeying the voice of the Angel, didst save Him from Herod's fury, *pray for the dying.*

St. Joseph, who, full of sorrow, with Mary didst seek Jesus for three days, *pray for the dying.*
St. Joseph, by whose labour He was fed, *pray for the dying.*
St. Joseph, guardian of the childhood and youth of Jesus, *pray for the dying.*
St. Joseph, who didst die in the arms of Jesus and Mary, *pray for the dying.*
St. Joseph, help of Christians in their last agony, *pray for the dying.*
St. Joseph, our protector and advocate with Jesus and Mary, *pray for the dying.*
Lamb of God, Who takest away the sins of the world, *spare us, O Lord.*
Lamb of God, Who takest away the sins of the world, *graciously hear us, O Lord.*
Lamb of God, Who takest away the sins of the world, *have mercy upon us, O Lord.*

V. Pray for us, holy Joseph,
R. That we may be made worthy of the promises of Christ.

Let us pray.

Pray for us, great Saint, and by thy love for Jesus and Mary, and by Their love for thee, obtain for us the happiness of living and dying in the love of Jesus and Mary. Amen.*

* *Manuel de la Confrérie du Cœur Agonisant,* pp. 57—60.

IV.

PRAYER OF A NUN OF THE VISITATION.

O HOLY Humanity of Jesus, let Thy infinite merits be applied to this poor soul now in its last agony, let Thy Precious Blood wash it, and fill it with Thy divine love.

Remember, O Lord Jesus, that this soul belongs to Thee, that Thou didst create it, didst regenerate it in holy baptism, didst redeem it by Thy painful death.

O Jesus, Who wast forsaken in Thine Agony in the Garden of Olives, help this poor soul, defend it from the enemies who are seeking its destruction.

O Almighty Jesus, rescue this soul from the hands of those who would take it from Thee. O Jesus, Brightness of the Eternal Glory, make this soul seek to glorify Thee. O my King, Thou hast given us the merit of all Thou didst suffer, let these merits avail for this poor soul, and save it from eternal death for the glory of Thy Name, and for the satisfaction of Thy Divine Heart, which is full of love for it. O most kind Jesus, by the merits of Thy Passion, grant to this soul, redeemed by Thee, the grace of a perfect conversion, and of final perseverance.

O Jesus, by Thy three hours' sad Agony on the Cross, mercifully give this soul grace to make sincere professions of faith, hope, and charity. O Divine Lamb, once sacrificed for us, make it humble, patient, and obedient; make it to forgive every offence, and to put away all resentment towards others; and fill it with heartfelt penitence for its offences against Thee, Thou Who art infinite goodness. O Jesus, my Saviour, by the desolation of Thy Heart, enable it to bear all desolation with peace, resignation, and love.

O Jesus, Thou knowest that I can do nothing, that this soul can do nothing without Thy grace. Grant us Thy grace, most merciful Redeemer.

O Jesus, Jesus, Jesus, be to it Jesus! Preserve it in the grace which Thou hast merited to obtain for us, be compassionate unto it, and receive it into the Wound in Thy Sacred Heart.

O Jesus, let this soul live only for Thee during its remaining moments. Let it die to live again eternally in Thee, the true Life.

O Jesus, let it listen to Thee if Thou dost speak, let it adore Thee if Thou art silent, let it be entirely submissive to Thy will.

O Jesus, defend and strengthen the dying heart, with faith, and grace, and trust in Thee.

O Jesus, Sacrifice of Propitiation, purify this soul in Thy Precious Blood.

O Jesus, let all Thy graces and mercies towards this soul work out its salvation, for Thine eternal glory, instead of showing Thy divine justice in its condemnation.

Let the burden of its sins, which deserve the punishment of death, fill it with a holy and loving fear; but let it see at the same time that the burden of the Cross which Thou didst bear has gained for it Heaven, and the eternal enjoyment of Thy love.

O Jesus, my Saviour, let this soul enter by the door of Thy Sacred Wounds, and appear spotless before Thy Heavenly Father, and let it have some of those holy feelings with which Thou didst die upon the Cross.

O Father, Son, and Holy Spirit, let the last act of the mortal life of this soul, now in agony, be an utterance of pure love of God. Let its last desire and strength be for Thee, and let it be inspired by the most ardent love. Let it make the sacrifice of life to Thee from a great desire of seeing Thee. Let it sigh after Thine eternal abode. Let it fly to Thee, borne upward by the flame of fervent love.

O Jesus, may it go with Thee to Calvary and the Cross, and from the Cross to Heaven. May its last sigh be in union with Thee.

O Jesus, Jesus, Jesus, show Thyself Jesus, and receive this soul into Thy Bosom. Amen.*

* *Vie de la dévote Sœur Jeanne Bénigne Gojos*, écrite par la Mère Marie-Gertrude Provare de Leyni, citée par Boulangé, *Manuel de la Confrérie du Cœur Agonisant*, pp. 64—69.

V.

PRAYER OF FATHER FRANCO.

O MOST gracious Jesus, Who at the sight of the multitude and of the enormity of our crimes, and of the fearful sufferings by which Thou wert about to expiate them, wast overwhelmed in the Garden of Olives by so great an Agony, that Thou didst pour forth a Sweat of Blood, by the cruel torments of Thine Heart, have mercy on Thy servant who is now in his last agony. By the weariness and sadness which Thou didst bear, soften the terrors of death for him; by the confidence which Thou hadst in Thy Heavenly Father, give him a firm hope in the divine mercy; by the Precious Blood which Thou didst shed from every part of Thy adorable Body, purify him from all his sins; and by the divine resignation with which Thou didst submit to Thy Father, make him accept of death with a perfect conformity to Thy holy will.*

VI.

PRAYERS OF MORVELLI.

O LORD JESUS, the refuge and helper of all sinners, we most earnestly beseech Thee, by

* Franco, *Nouveau Manuel de la dévotion au Sacré Cœur de Jésus*, pt. 2, Prières pour les Agonisants.

Thine Agony, by Thy most holy Prayer to Thy Father on the Mount of Olives, and by Thy Sweat of Blood, mercifully to offer to Thy Divine Father all the anguish and distress Thou didst then suffer for the many sins of this His creature, now in his last agony. We pray thee, O Lord, to deliver him in the awful hour of death from all pains and sorrows, which he fears he may have to undergo for his sins.

O Thou sweetest rest of our souls and bodies, Jesus, Son of God, Lord and Saviour of the human race, in the night of Thy Passion Thou didst say in Thy Prayer to Thy Father: "My Father, if it be possible, let this chalice pass from Me. Nevertheless, not as I wilt, but as Thou wilt." At that hour Thy Anguish was so great, that a Sweat of Blood poured from Thy whole Body. We beseech Thee, most merciful Lord, give us grace to call upon Thee so earnestly for this sick person, who is about to give up his soul to Thee, that we may be worthy to obtain for him the forgiveness of all his sins.

O most merciful Lord, consolation of the world, joy of Angels and of men, how fearful was Thy state in the Garden of Olives, when Thy Agony and mortal sadness caused Thee to pour forth a Sweat of Blood. Thou didst need an Angel to comfort Thee, Thou wast constrained to pray that Thy Father would let that bitter chalice pass; yet, resigned to that Father's will, Thou didst say, "Not My will, but Thine be done!" Now, by Thy Blood, by Thine Agony, by the mortal anguish Thou didst suffer so humbly, we pray Thee to perform the office of the Angel of Consolation for this agonising soul, to strengthen it amid the horrors and pains of death, so that with Thee it may say, "O Eternal Father, I am content, not my will, but Thine be done."*

VII.

PRAYERS OF LATTAIGNANT.

O MOST sweet Lord Jesus Christ, Who on the night of Thy Passion didst pray to Thy Father, saying, "Remove this chalice from Me; but yet not My will, but Thine be done;" the sadness and the fear, the weariness and the pain which Thou didst then undergo were so great that thy Sweat was as drops of Blood, trickling down upon the ground. O good Jesus, by this sadness, by these fears, by this weariness, by that Sweat of Blood, we beseech Thee to strengthen the soul of this Thy servant who is suffering, to give him the consolation, the grace, and the strength he now so greatly needs.

O most kind Jesus, Divine Shepherd of Souls,

---

* Morvelli, *Apparecchio dell' anima per il felice passagio all' altra vita*, p. 237, 239, 277.

Who on the night of Thy Passion wast forsaken by Thy Disciples, and left in the hands of Thine enemies; we most humbly pray Thee not to leave this poor soul in the hands of its enemies and Thine; but mercifully to lead it into the place of eternal rest by the merits of Thy most holy Passion.

O most kind Lord Jesus Christ, Who didst feel in the person of Judas how great a grief it is to have a faithless friend, do not let this soul be faithless to Thee, do not let it lose Thy love, as he did. The glory of Thy love is in making sinners holy, and traitors faithful; if ever this soul has been among the number of Thy betrayers, convert it and make it faithful to Thee even unto death. Amen.*

VIII.

LITANY OF THE DYING.

LORD have mercy on him (*or* her).
Christ have mercy on him.
Lord have mercy on him.
Holy Mary, *pray for him* [or *her*].
All ye holy Angels and Archangels, *pray for him.*
Holy Abel, *pray for him.*

---

* De Lattaignant, *Les Secours spirituels que l'on doit au prochain dans les maladies qui pennent aller à la mort,* n. 16.

PRAYERS FOR THE DYING. 247

All ye choirs of the Just, *pray for him*.
Holy Abraham, *pray for him*.
St. John Baptist, *pray for him*.
St. Joseph, *pray for him*.
All ye holy Patriarchs and Prophets, *pray for him*.
St. Peter, *pray for him*.
St. Paul, *pray for him*.
St. Andrew, *pray for him*.
St. John, *pray for him*.
All ye holy Apostles and Evangelists, *pray for him*.
All ye holy Disciples of our Lord, *pray for him*.
All ye holy Innocents, *pray for him*.
St. Stephen, *pray for him*.
St. Lawrence, *pray for him*.
All ye holy Martyrs, *pray for him*.
St. Sylvester, *pray for him*.
St. Gregory, *pray for him*.
St. Augustine, *pray for him*.
All ye holy Bishops and Confessors, *pray for him*.
St. Benedict, *pray for him*.
St. Francis, *pray for him*.
All ye holy Monks and Hermits, *pray for him*.
St. Mary Magdalen, *pray for him*.
St. Lucy, *pray for him*.
All ye holy Virgins and Widows, *pray for him*.
All ye men and women, Saints of God, *intercede for him* [or *her*].
Be merciful unto him, O God. *Spare him, O Lord.*
Be merciful unto him. *Deliver him* [or *her*], *O Lord.*

Be merciful unto him. *Deliver him* [or *her*], *O Lord.*
From Thy wrath, *deliver him, O Lord.*
From the danger of eternal death, *deliver him, O Lord.*
From an evil death, *deliver him, O Lord.*
From the pains of hell, *deliver him, O Lord.*
From all evil, *deliver him, O Lord.*
From the power of the devil, *deliver him, O Lord.*
By Thy Nativity, *deliver him, O Lord.*
By Thy Cross ✠ and Passion, *deliver him, O Lord.*
By Thy Death and Burial, *deliver him, O Lord.*
By Thy glorious Resurrection, *deliver him, O Lord.*
By Thy wonderful Ascension, *deliver him, O Lord.*
By the grace of the Holy Ghost the Comforter, *deliver him, O Lord.*
In the day of Judgment, *deliver him, O Lord.*
We sinners, *beseech Thee to hear us.*
That Thou spare him, *we beseech Thee to hear us.*
Lord have mercy on him.
Christ have mercy on him.
Lord have mercy on him.

IX.

RECOMMENDATION OF A DEPARTING SOUL.

Go forth, O Christian soul, out of this world, in the name of God the Father Almighty, Who created thee; in the name of Jesus Christ, the Son of the living God, Who suffered for thee;

in the name of the Holy Ghost, Who sanctified thee; in the name of the Angels, Archangels, Thrones, and Dominations, Cherubim and Seraphim; in the name of the Patriarchs and Prophets, of the holy Apostles and Evangelists, of the holy Martyrs, Confessors, Monks and Hermits, of the holy Virgins, and of all the Saints of God. May thy place be this day in peace, and thy abode in holy Sion. Through Christ our Lord. Amen.

O merciful and gracious God, O God, Who according to the multitude of Thy mercies blottest out the sins of such as repent, and graciously remittest the guilt of their past offences, mercifully regard this Thy servant, N., and grant him [or her] a full discharge from all his sins, who with a contrite heart most earnestly begs it of Thee. Renew, O merciful Father, whatever has been vitiated in him, by human frailty, or by the frauds and deceits of the enemy; and associate him as a member of redemption to the unity of the body of the Church. Have compassion, O Lord, on his sighs, have compassion on his tears, and admit him, who has no hope but in Thy mercy, to the sacrament of Thy reconciliation. Through Christ our Lord. Amen.

I commend Thee, dear brother, to the Almighty God, and consign thee to the care of Him, whose creature thou art, that, when thou shalt have paid the debt of all mankind by death, thou mayest return to thy Maker, Who formed thee from the dust of the earth. When, therefore, thy soul shall depart from thy body, may the resplendent multitude of the Angels meet thee; may the court of the Apostles receive thee; may the triumphant army of glorious Martyrs come out to welcome thee; may the splendid company of Confessors clad in their white robes encompass thee; may the choir of joyful Virgins receive thee; and mayest thou meet with a blessed repose in the bosom of the Patriarchs. May Jesus Christ appear to thee with a mild and joyful countenance, and appoint thee a place amongst those who are to stand before Him for ever. Mayest thou be a stranger to all that is punished with darkness, chastised with flames, and condemned to torments. May the most wicked enemy, with all his evil spirits, be forced to give way; may he tremble at thy approach in the company of Angels, and with confusion fly away into the vast chaos of eternal night. Let God arise and His enemies be dispersed, and let them that hate Him fly before His face, let them vanish like smoke; and as wax that melts before the fire, so let sinners perish in the sight of God; but may the just rejoice and be happy in His presence. May then all the legions of hell be confounded and put to shame; and may none of the ministers of Satan dare to stop thee in thy way. May Christ deliver thee from torments,

Who was crucified for thee. May He deliver thee from eternal death, Who vouchsafed to die for thee. May Jesus Christ, the Son of the living God, place thee in the ever-verdant lawns of His Paradise; and may He, the true Shepherd, acknowledge thee for one of His flock. May He absolve thee from all thy sins, and place thee at His right hand in the midst of His Elect. Mayest thou see thy Redeemer face to face, and, standing always in His presence, behold with happy eyes the most clear truth. And mayest thou be placed among the companies of the Blessed, and enjoy the sweetness of the contemplation of thy God for ever. Amen.

V. Receive, O Lord, Thy servant into the place of salvation, which he hopes to obtain through Thy mercy.
R. Amen.
V. Deliver, O Lord, the soul of Thy servant from all danger of hell, and from all pain and tribulation.
R. Amen.
V. Deliver, O Lord, the soul of Thy servant, as Thou deliveredst Enoch and Elias from the common death of the world.
R. Amen.
V. Deliver, O Lord, the soul of Thy servant, as Thou deliveredst Noah from the flood.
R. Amen.

V. Deliver, O Lord, the soul of Thy servant, as Thou deliveredst Abraham from the midst of the Chaldeans.
R. Amen.
V. Deliver, O Lord, the soul of Thy servant, as Thou deliveredst Job from all his afflictions.
R. Amen.
V. Deliver, O Lord, the soul of Thy servant, as Thou deliveredst Isaac from being sacrificed by his father.
R. Amen.
V. Deliver, O Lord, the soul of Thy servant, as Thou deliveredst Lot from being destroyed in the flames of Sodom.
R. Amen.
V. Deliver, O Lord, the soul of Thy servant, as Thou deliveredst Moses from the hands of Pharaoh, King of Egypt.
R. Amen.
V. Deliver, O Lord, the soul of Thy servant, as Thou deliveredst Daniel from the lions' den.
R. Amen.
V. Deliver, O Lord, the soul of Thy servant, as Thou deliveredst the Three Children from the fiery furnace, and from the hands of an unmerciful King.
R. Amen.
V. Deliver, O Lord, the soul of Thy servant, as Thou deliveredst Susanna from her false accusers.
R. Amen.

V. Deliver, O Lord, the soul of Thy servant, as Thou deliveredst David from the hands of Saul and Goliah.

R. Amen.

V. Deliver, O Lord, the soul of Thy servant, as Thou deliveredst Peter and Paul out of prison.

R. Amen.

V. And as Thou deliveredst that blessed Virgin and Martyr, St. Thecla, from three most cruel torments, so vouchsafe to deliver the soul of this Thy servant, and bring it to the participation of Thy heavenly joys.

R. Amen.

We commend to Thee, O Lord, the soul of Thy servant, N., and we beseech Thee, O Lord Jesus Christ, the Saviour of the world, that as in mercy to him Thou becamest Man, so now Thou wouldst vouchsafe to admit him to the bosom of Thy Patriarchs. Remember, O Lord, he is Thy creature, not made by strange gods, but by Thee, the only living and true God; for there is no other God but Thee, and none that can equal Thy works. Let his soul rejoice in Thy presence, and remember not his former iniquities and excesses, which he has fallen into through the violence of passion and the corruption of his nature. For although he has sinned, yet he has always firmly believed in the Father, Son, and Holy Ghost; he has had a zeal for Thy honour, and faithfully adored Thee as his God, and the Creator of all things.

Remember not, O Lord, we beseech Thee, the sins of his youth and his ignorances, but, according to Thy great mercy, be mindful of him in Thy heavenly glory. Let the Heavens be opened to him, and the Angels rejoice with him. Let the Archangel St. Michael, whom Thou hast appointed the chief of the heavenly host, conduct him. Let the holy Angels come out to meet him, and carry him to the city of the heavenly Jerusalem. Let blessed Peter the Apostle, to whom God gave the keys of the Kingdom of Heaven, receive him. Let St. Paul the Apostle, who was a vessel of election, assist him. Let St. John, the Beloved Disciple, to whom the secrets of Heaven were revealed, intercede for him. Let all the holy Apostles, who received from Jesus Christ the power of binding and loosing, pray for him. Let all the Saints and Elect of God, who in this world have suffered torments for the name of Christ, intercede for him; that being freed from the prison of his body, he may be admitted into the glory of Thy Heavenly Kingdom. Through the grace and merits of our Lord Jesus Christ, Who with Thee and the Holy Ghost, liveth and reigneth one God, world without end.

R. Amen.

The soul being departed, the following Responsary may be said:—

Come to his [*or* her] assistance, all ye Saints of God; meet him, all ye Angels of God: receiving his soul, offering it in the sight of the Most High. May Christ receive thee, Who hath called thee, and may the Angels conduct thee to Abraham's bosom. Receiving his soul and offering it in the sight of the Most High.

V. Eternal rest give to him, O Lord, and let perpetual light shine upon him.
R. Offering it in the sight of the Most High.
V. Lord have mercy on him.
R. Christ have mercy on him.
V. Lord have mercy on him.
Our Father, &c.
V. And lead us not into temptation.
R. But deliver us from evil.
V. Eternal rest give to him, O Lord.
R. And let perpetual light shine upon him.
V. From the gates of hell,
R. Deliver his soul, O Lord.
V. May he rest in peace.
R. Amen.
V. O Lord, hear my prayer.
R. And let my supplication come unto Thee.

Let us pray.

To Thee, O Lord, we commend the soul of Thy servant, N., that being dead to this world he may live to Thee; and whatever sins he has committed in this life through human frailty, do Thou in Thy most merciful goodness forgive. Through our Lord Jesus Christ. Amen.

Works Published by Burns, Oates, and Co.

New Book for Holy Communion.

REFLECTIONS AND PRAYERS FOR HOLY COMMUNION. Translated from the French. Fcp., cloth, 8vo. Uniform with *Imitation of the Sacred Heart.* With Preface by Archbishop Manning. Cloth, 4s. 6d.; bound, red edges, 5s.; calf, 8s.; morocco, 9s.

New Book of Meditations for Religious, or for Persons in the World.

THE DAY SANCTIFIED: being Meditations and Spiritual Readings for Daily use. Selected from the Works of Saints and approved writers of the Catholic Church. Fcp., cloth, 3s. 6d.; red edges, 4s.

Of the many volumes of meditation on sacred subjects which have appeared in the last few years, none has seemed to us so well adapted to its object as the one before us.—*Tablet.*
Deserves to be specially mentioned.—*Month.*
Admirable in every sense.—*Church Times.*
Many of the meditations are of great beauty. . . . They form, in fact, excellent little sermons, and we have no doubt will be largely used as such.—*Literary Churchman.*

Now ready.

THE LIFE OF B. MARGARET MARY ALACOQUE. By the Rev. G. Tickell, S.J. Demy 8vo, handsome cloth, 7s. 6d.

In neat cloth, 3s. 6d.

OUR FATHER: Popular Discourses on the Lord's Prayer. By Dr. Emanuel Veith, Preacher in Ordinary in the Cathedral of Vienna. (Dr. V. is one of the most eminent preachers on the Continent.)

Works Published by Burns, Oates, and Co.

Now ready.

PART II. OF SERMONS BY FATHERS OF THE SOCIETY OF JESUS.

CONTENTS.—I. The Angelus Bell: Five Lectures on the Remedies against Desolation and Despondency. By Father Gallwey.—II. The Infancy of our Lord. Three Sermons by Father Parkinson.

The contents of this volume will be found useful for Religious Communities and persons wishing to lead a spiritual life.

PART I., by Fathers Coleridge and Hathaway. Fcp. 8vo, 2s.

Shortly.

PART III. Miscellaneous Sermons, by various authors.

Now ready.

THE DAY HOURS OF THE CHURCH. Cloth, 1s.

Also, separately,

THE OFFICES OF PRIME AND COMPLINE. 8d.
THE OFFICES OF TIERCE, SEXT, AND NONE. 3d.

Now ready, fcp. 8vo, price 4s.

DISCOURSES ON SOME PARABLES of the NEW TESTAMENT. By the Rev. G. B. Garside.

LIFE OF HENRY DORIE, MARTYR. Translated by Lady Herbert. 1s.; cloth, 1s. 6d.

Works Published by Burns, Oates, and Co.

Just out, price 1s.

JOAN OF ARC. By Mgr. Felix, Bishop of Orleans. A Discourse delivered on May 8, 1869, in the Cathedral of Holy Cross, Orleans. Translated by Emily Bowles.

Now ready, fcp. 8vo, 3s.

THE HIDDEN LIFE OF JESUS: A Lesson and Model to Christians. Translated from the French of Henri-Marie Boudon, Archdeacon of Evreux, by Edward Healy Thompson, M.A.

Now ready, price 3s. Suitable for Michaelmas and the month of October.

DEVOTION to the NINE CHOIRS of HOLY ANGELS, and especially to the Angel Guardians. Translated from the French of Henri-Marie Boudon, Archdeacon of Evreux, by Edward Healy Thompson, M.A.

Now ready, neat cloth, 3s. 6d.; cloth elegant, with Frontispiece, 4s. 6d.; also, a fine-paper Edition, calf, 10s., and morocco, 12s.

THE GLORIES OF MARY. Translated from the Italian of St. Alphonsus Liguori. New and complete edition. Revised by the Very Rev. Father Coffin.

Just out, neat cloth, red edges, 1s.; calf, 4s.

MARY IN SORROW AND DESOLATION, Help of the Catholic Church. With the Ritual of the Confraternity of Our Lady of Dolours.

Works Published by Burns, Oates, and Co.

FAMILY DEVOTIONS (Liturgical) for every Day in the Week. Selected from Catholic Manuals, ancient and modern. Fcp., limp cloth, red edges, very neat, 2s.

POPULAR DEVOTIONS FOR THE ECCLESIASTICAL SEASONS: being short Evening Services of Psalms, Prayers, and Hymns, suited for singing. In Numbers, complete in one vol., cloth, 1s.; also, in Nos. at 2d. each.

Contains: 1. Devotions for Advent and Christmas. 2. Devotions from Septuagesima to Easter. 3. Devotions for Paschal Time. 4. Devotions for Whitsuntide. 5. Devotions for the Sundays after Pentecost. 6. Devotions for the Feasts of the Blessed Virgin. 7. Devotions for Saints' Days.

*** Music for these Devotions, complete, 1s. 6d.

MANUAL OF THE CROSS AND PASSION of our LORD JESUS CHRIST. By Father Sebastian, Priest of the Order of Passionists. Bound in strong cloth, toned paper, 3s.; bevelled covers, gilt edges, 4s. 6d.; morocco, 7s. 6d.

Just ready, price 6s.

LIFE OF BLESSED CHARLES SPINOLA, S.J. By Father Brockeart, S.J.

Now ready,

HOLY CONFIDENCE. By Father Rogacci, of the Society of Jesus. One vol. 18mo, cloth, 2s.

Works Published by Burns, Oates, and Co.

Burns and Co.'s new 2s. universal prayer-book. A marvel of cheapness! More than 1,000 pages for 2s. Thirty-second thousand.

THE PATH TO HEAVEN: The Cheapest and most Complete Book of Devotions for Public or Private Use ever issued. Cloth lettered, 2s.; neatly bound, red edges, 2s. 6d.; neatly bound, clasp and rim, 4s.; roan, lettered, 3s.; roan, full gilt, clasp, 4s. 6d.; French morocco, gilt edges, 4s.; calf, red edges, 5s.; best calf, tooled, 7s. 6d.; morocco, 6s.; morocco, gilt, 7s.; do., gilt extra, 8s.; do., rim and clasp, 12s.; do., gilt, ivory rim and clasp, 14s.; velvet, rim and clasp, 10s. 6d.; best Turkey morocco, 8s. 6d.; do. gilt, 10s.

CATHOLIC'S VADE MECUM; a Pocket Manual of Prayer for daily use. Beautifully printed in a clear type on fine thin paper, and in limp binding; does not exceed 4½ oz. in weight. Price, in cloth, 2s.; roan, 2s. 6d.; Fr. morocco, 3s. 6d.; calf, red edges, 4s.; morocco plain, 4s. 6d.; gilt, 5s. 6d. Also, antique style, morocco and velvet, 12s. to 21s.; antique, photographic illustrations, clasp, for presents, 25s., 30s., &c.; ivory, elegantly ornamented, 21s.

A MANUAL FOR SERVING-BOYS. Edited by the Rev. R. W. Brundrit, M.A. Neat cloth, 6d.; wrapper, 4d.

NEW VISITS TO THE BLESSED SACRAMENT. Edited by Cardinal Wiseman. 1s. 6d.; or with frontispiece, bound in cloth gilt, 2s.; morocco, elegant, 5s.

Works Published by Burns, Oates, and Co.

GOLDEN MANUAL (The); or Complete Guide to Devotion, Public or Private. New edition, enlarged and improved, 800 pages. Embossed gilt edges, 5s. 6d.; calf, flexible back, very neat and durable, 7s. 6d.; morocco plain, 8s. 6d.; gilt, 10s. Also bound for presents in elegant bindings, with antique boards and edges, clasps, corners, &c., 21s. and upwards; ivory, beautifully ornamented, 42s.; velvet rims and clasp, very elegant, 24s.

Also an edition on fine thin satin paper, *one inch thick*. Calf, 7s. 6d.; morocco, 8s. 6d.; gilt, 10s.; limp morocco, edges turned over, 12s.

The same, with Epistles and Gospels, calf, 8s. 6d.; morocco, 9s. 6d.; gilt, 11s.

THE NEW TESTAMENT NARRATIVE, in the Words of the Sacred Writers. With Notes, Chronological Tables, and Maps. A book for those who, as a matter of education or of devotion, wish to be thoroughly well acquainted with the life of our Lord. What is narrated by each of His Evangelists is woven into a continuous and chronological narrative. Thus the study of the Gospels is complete and yet easy. Cloth, 2s. 6d.

> The compilers deserve great praise for the manner in which they have performed their task. We commend this little volume as well and carefully printed, and as furnishing its readers, moreover, with a great amount of useful information in the tables inserted in the end.—*Month.*
> It is at once clear, complete, and beautiful."—*Catholic Opinion.*

LIGUORI (St.) Visits to the B. Sacrament and to the B. V. Mary. An entirely new translation by the Redemptorist Fathers. 1s. cloth; bound, roan, 1s. 6d.; Fr. morocco, 2s. 6d.; calf, 4s.; morocco plain, 4s. 6d.; morocco gilt, 5s. 6d.

Works Published by Burns, Oates, and Co.

LIGUORI (St. Alphonso). New and improved Translation of the Complete Works of St. Alphonso, edited by Father Coffin.
Vol. I. The Christian Virtues, and the means for obtaining them. Cloth elegant, 4s.—Or, separately: (1.) The Love of our Lord Jesus Christ, 1s. 4d. (2.) Treatise on Prayer, 1s. 4d. (*In the ordinary editions a great part of this work is omitted*). (3.) A Christian's Rule of Life, 1s.
Vol. II. The Mysteries of the Faith—the Incarnation; containing Meditations and Devotions on the Birth and Infancy of Jesus Christ, &c. Suited for Advent and Christmas. 3s. 6d. Cheap edition, 2s.
Vol. III. The Mysteries of the Faith—the Blessed Sacrament. 3s. 6d. Cheap edition, 2s.
Vol. IV. Eternal Truths — Preparation for Death. 3s. 6d. Cheap edition, 2s.
Vol. V. Treatises on the Passion. Containing, "Jesus hath loved us," &c. 3s. Cheap edition, 2s.
Vol. VI. Glories of Mary. New edition. 3s. 6d.; with Frontispiece, cloth elegant, 4s. 6d.
St. Liguori's "Jesus hath Loved us," separately; *new and correct edition*, 9d. cloth.

VESPER BOOK FOR THE LAITY. This volume contains the Office of Vespers (including Compline and Benediction) complete for the first time for *every day in the year*, with the New Offices and Supplements. Roan, gilt edges, 3s. 6d.; calf, 5s. 6d.; morocco, 6s. 6d.; gilt, 7s. 6d. The same, in thin vellum, half an inch thick, same prices.

LIFE OF ST. THOMAS OF CANTERBURY. By Mrs. Hope, author of the *Early Martyrs*. Cloth extra, 4s. 6d. With Preface by Father Dalgairns.

Works Published by Burns, Oates, and Co.

Just published, price 2s. 6d.

THE CHURCH OF ST. PATRICK: or, a History of the Origin, Doctrines, Liturgy, and Governmental System of the Ancient Church of Ireland. With supplementary observations on the necessity of an amelioration of the condition of Irish Catholicism. By the Rev. William Waterworth, S.J.

A lucid and well-written treatise.—*Tablet.*
It is written with much force and vigour, and is very pleasant reading.—*Month.*

Narratives of Missions.

THE COREAN MARTYRS. By Canon Shortland. Cloth, 2s.

A narrative of Missions and Martyrdoms too little known in this country.

MANUAL OF THE THIRD ORDER of St. Francis. Complete, with the Devotions. In two vols., 18mo, cloth, 6s.

www.ingramcontent.com/pod-product-compliance
Lightning Source LLC
Chambersburg PA
CBHW032101220426